This . . .

Being part of a crowd hoping for a handout from the Red Cross...

or this?

Being prepared and enjoying good water from your own water filter.

You choose.

What others are saying about this book

"Thank you for the recently shipped additional copy of Do-It-Yourself Emergency Preparedness. I was part of a medical team deployed to the area in the immediate disaster aftermath of Hurricanes Katrina and Rita. The information provided by this book proved invaluable for those of us providing services with limited resources and those unprepared local citizens anxiously affected by the events.

"As the cascade of tragic events from water, food and fuel shortages developed into concerns of civil unrest and personal security, the calm reassuring words **'You are fine. It's all in the book—we are prepared'** came to receptive ears. They are all believers now.

"I have since given all seven of my family members (all affected by the storms) copies of your book. When we discuss the many tragic events that transpired and discuss preparing for future scenarios, we simply say 'it's in the book.'

"Do-It-Yourself Emergency Preparedness is a must-have for anyone desiring to step out of the unprepared world of denial and invest in the security of critically useful knowledge. Thank you for the time and energy that will benefit so many through this book."

— T. B. P., MD

"With 25 years in emergency services I have read hundreds of manuals, pamphlets, magazines, books, and articles.

"I just finished Do-It-Yourself Emergency Preparedness. Quite simply, it is the best how-to book on emergency preparedness I have ever read. It is easy to read, touches all the bases, and if followed, will assist you and your loved ones not only to survive, but to do so in relative comfort."

—R. GEBO,
Captain, Foothill Fire Protection District

"A great step-by-step guide to getting motivated and prepared for an emergency. Interesting and engaging. Arlene Hoag brings the 'What If' question to life with real-life situations. Outstanding sections on food and water storage, power generation, communication and biological terrorism."

—L. MALIN,
Major Surplus & Survival Book Dept. Manager

"For those, like myself, who cannot claim to be an expert in emergency management and disaster preparedness, I found the information contained to be easy to understand and very informative. Do-It-Yourself Emergency Preparedness *provides solutions that invite the reader to prepare, avoiding the need to focus on one's ignorance or fears. I plan to use this book as a resource for my own planning and preparation for possible, if not eventual, disasters."*

—T. EDWARDS,
Salt Lake City, UT

*"*Do-It-Yourself Emergency Preparedness *is THE definitive preparedness guide. The scenarios presented in this book are timely and accurate, and the suggestions provide practical and sensible solutions to help prepare yourself and your family for many emergencies. This book belongs in every home library."*

—C. CLARK
New Hampshire

"My compliments on your new book on preparedness. It's simple, well put together and easy to understand."

—O. RILEY,
Riley Stove Company

"In Toronto last week there were over 70,000 people without power for 72 hours. What a coincidence! Your book arrived just in time to help. Water and food were the first things on your list and so I made sure to have plenty of both on hand. I had not updated the batteries on two of our flashlights so they died after about an hour but we had lots of candles so we made do. One of the things that your book talks about is a wood burning stove and though we have considered it in the past, after three days with no electricity, it has moved to the top of the 'Things to do' list.

"Your book was well organized and full of useful information. It contained plenty of helpful tips and covered all the major topics from food storage to emergency rations to power generation. The writing style is straightforward and easy to follow and would be an asset to any library. I continue to reference the book daily as I have been recently updating my 72-hour emergency kit. Thank you for your much-needed contribution to this topic and I am sure this book will help people all over the world."

—J. WONTA,
Canada

"We provide financial preparedness support for our clients. In addition, we offer non-financial preparedness services. After reviewing three dozen books on this subject, we chose the book, Do-It-Yourself Emergency Preparedness, *as the most useful resource. We especially appreciated the fact that this book approached emergency preparedness from a very practical, balanced viewpoint. Great job!"*

—J. MCDERMOTT,
Founder
LaSalle St. Securities, LLC
Elmhurst, IL

Do-It-Yourself
Emergency Preparedness
How Ordinary People Prepare for Extra-Ordinary Events

Do-It-Yourself
Emergency Preparedness
How Ordinary People Prepare for Extra-Ordinary Events

by Arlene R. Hoag

Yellowstone River Publishing
Bozeman, Montana
United States of America

DO-IT-YOURSELF EMERGENCY PREPAREDNESS
How Ordinary People Prepare for Extra-Ordinary Events
by Arlene Hoag
Copyright © 2007 by Arlene R. Hoag.
All rights reserved

Cover illustration and design, and chapter title page
artwork by Roxanne Duke

For information contact:
Yellowstone River Publishing
1716 S. Willson Ave.
Bozeman, Montana 59715.
Tel: 406-223-4707
E-mail: orders1@yellowstonetrading.com
Web site: www.yellowstonetrading.com

Printed in the United States of America.

10   09   08   07   06   5   4   3   2   1

To all those who
yearn for hope and peace of mind
in these distressing times

Table of Contents

Acknowledgments

I would like to acknowledge the support and assistance of the many individuals, named and unnamed, who have contributed to the completion of this book. I offer deep gratitude to Alyssa Angelis for your enthusiastic work of typesetting and layout; to Alan Engelbart for your personal support of this project as well as all of your website expertise; to Robert Gluckson for your endless hours of copyediting and offering helpful suggestions all along the way; to Roxanne Duke for your beautiful artwork, cover design and for your encouragement over the past ten years; to my daughter Bethany Orr for taking care of the Yellowstone Trading business so that there was time to put together this new book, to my sons Brian and Jonathan for helping so much in the computer and web site areas, and to my younger sons, Jesse and David, for enriching our lives in so many ways.

I would like to offer thanks to all our friends and family who have supported us throughout the different stages of this project and who have confirmed for us the need for this type of information at this particular time. Finally, thanks to all our readers of No Such Thing as Doomsday *who have shown us their appreciation for the helpful information they found in that book.*

Introduction

Everyday life involves making decisions and taking risks. Risk is found both in action and inaction. How much impact do you think a particular calamity could have on you and your family? We all have to decide to either prepare or not to prepare. Are you willing to wager the comfort, health and life of your family on a bet that nothing unpleasant is going to occur in the future? Or do you want to stack the odds in your family's favor through an investment in preparedness?

Preparing for a possible emergency is just good common sense, like having a spare tire in your trunk, buying insurance on your house, or wearing a seat belt. Preparedness is a form of alternative life insurance. This type of policy doesn't pay a financial dividend; but in time of natural or man-made disaster, it could provide a priceless return. It can insure the well-being of your family.

By securing a copy of this book, you have already begun your preparedness plans. The investment in preparedness starts with simply your attention. You decide you are going to get ready for a possible, unforeseen emergency. After that, a small investment of your time and resources is all that is needed. Many of the things you need in an emergency you may already have. You just need to gather them up, organize them and keep them accessible. Thinking about these items ahead of time is the key. Have you ever noticed how difficult it is to think in the midst of a crisis?

In the midst of a crisis is the time for action. *Before* the crisis is the best time for thinking.

You can prepare and this book will be an immense help, a reference guide both before and during a disaster. Even if you do nothing now, there is a chapter specifically on what to do when an emergency starts which succinctly covers the key points to be considered at this critical time.

Do-It-Yourself Emergency Preparedness is the definitive guide through any disaster or emergency. Learn how to prepare for these situations:

- No electricity in your area for three weeks

- A hurricane which necessitates evacuation

- A biological terrorist attack where the air becomes unsafe

- Extreme weather patterns that disrupt the growing cycle and availability of food

- An earthquake that devastates your area

Our previous book, *No Such Thing as Doomsday,* is the definitive text for the seriously survival-minded who plan to build an underground or basement shelter. *Do-It-Yourself Emergency Preparedness* grew out of a desire to create a book as informative and useful as our previous book yet smaller, more economical and with an appeal to a much wider audience. This book doesn't spend much time describing potential threats—what you want now are the solutions.

Throughout this book we make suggestions regarding items you can secure that will help you to get prepared and, in many cases, the sources for these items. Our hope is that the effort we have invested in producing this book will save *you* considerable effort. Our goal is to help you move from a state of worry about the future to having the peace of mind that comes from knowing you have done your best to get ready for whatever may come.

CHAPTER 1
Steps to Take when an Emergency Starts

If you have just bought this book and a disaster strikes tomorrow, this section will help. If you have bought this book and things have been so busy for the last six months that you have not had a chance to read it yet and a disaster strikes tomorrow, this section will help. If you have bought this book, read it and completed many of the preparations and a disaster strikes tomorrow, this section may help because it can remind you of the essential elements to consider in an emergency.

Step 1

Determine if it is safe to remain in your house.

A. If you know you need to evacuate, turn to the chapter on evacuation titled "If You Need to Leave Your Home" and quickly gather as many things on the checklist for a 72-hour survival pack as you can. Leave as quickly as possible. Drive in your car if you can. Walk if you need to.

B. You may decide that it is unsafe to remain in your house because it is unstable structurally due to whatever damage has happened in the disaster, yet it would be safe to stay in the vicinity (i.e., your yard, a nearby park).

1. Check your house for any gas smell. If you smell leaking gas, turn off the gas if you can. Propane can be turned off easily by shutting off the knob on the top of the tank. It can be turned back on just as easily. Natural gas requires a special tool to turn it off. If you have natural gas it would be very helpful to own one of these tools. However, only turn off the gas if you smell a leak. The gas company has to come out to turn the gas back on. They will undoubtedly be very busy during and after an emergency. If you have gas heat and it's wintertime, this could present a problem.

2. Consider what your options are for alternative shelter. A tent would be the first choice. Rope and a tarp or plastic would also work. (Securing a small rock with string into each corner of the tarp or the piece of plastic will allow you to more easily tie the corners to the ground or to a tree.) If you have to make a shelter out of branches, sticks, etc., use your creativity. Children would be a great asset in this situation as they are naturals at building forts. If the weather is mild, building a shelter would not be as important a consideration as water and food.

Tying a small rock in the corner of a tarp or plastic sheet makes it much easier to construct a sturdy shelter.

Step 2

Your house is still suitable to shelter you but you have no electricity.

A. If there is still water coming out of the pipes, fill up as many containers as possible with water. Unless you have reason to suspect that the water may be contaminated, it should be fine to drink as is. Do not use your water for flushing toilets or washing until you have stored adequate drinking and cooking water. Even if you have water pressure now, if there is no electricity in your area, it is likely you will not continue to have running water. Store as much water as possible (one gallon per person per day) and conserve. For more information, see the chapter on water.

B. Take inventory of what food you have. You may not be able to count on going to the store. If you have an abundance of one kind of food, you may be able to trade with a neighbor for something you don't have. Soaking grains and beans cuts down on cooking time. Plan one or two meals now. Don't wait until everyone is really hungry to think about the next meal. For more information, see the chapter on food.

C. How will you cook your food? Is your stove working? If not, possible alternatives are a barbecue, camping stove or wood stove. For more information, see the chapter on heating and cooking.

D. Do you need heat to keep warm? Even if you have gas heat, it probably won't work if the electricity is off. Gather up extra clothes and blankets. Try to keep yourself comfortably warm. Don't wait until you are really cold and stiff to put on extra clothes. For more information, see the chapter on heating and cooking.

E. If it is daytime, find working flashlights, candles, light sticks or kerosene lamps now, while you can see. Locate the matches. For more information, see the chapter on lighting.

F. Are the phones working? What about your cell phone? Having an older phone that doesn't need electricity to operate could be very valuable. If you don't have a way to communicate by phone, maybe someone in your neighborhood does.

G. Do you have a radio that works without electricity, (batteries, solar, wind-up)? If so, turn it on and get information on the disaster. This can be extremely helpful in knowing what to expect so you can be better prepared. If you don't have a working radio, maybe a neighbor does. For more information, see the chapter on communication.

Step 3

Relax yet stay focused. If you need to take a break from your preparations or you have some free time, read the rest of this book.

CHAPTER 2

Peace of Mind through Preparedness Checklist

Great! You've decided it makes sense to get ready in case disaster of any sort strikes in your community. Here is a list of things you can begin gathering that will help you to maintain a degree of comfort through any emergency. Consider preparing at three levels: a) minimum, b) adequate, or c) ideal.

1. Drinking Water

a) Minimum: Store at least one gallon of water per person per day, with a three-day minimum. This can be used for cooking as well as drinking. Check and replenish your stored water at least every six months.

A bottle of water treatment tablets will allow you to change questionable quality water into drinkable water.

b) Adequate: Have a portable water filter so if you run out of stored water or have to evacuate, you will be ready.

c) Ideal: Purchase an AquaRain gravity feed water filter (no electricity needed). This will provide drinkable water from any surface water source.

2. Emergency Food

a) Minimum: Store canned food and staples such as beans, rice and noodles. Buy one extra every time you go to the grocery store. Have a non-electric can opener. Have a camping stove or barbecue available for cooking.

b) Adequate: Get a one-week supply of AlpineAire food (minimal or no cooking required) for each member of your family. Have a way to heat water.

c) Ideal: Buy a larger long-term food package. These have a shelf life of 10+ years. You won't need to be concerned about these foods getting too old to use. Get a reliable camp stove.

3. Light

a) Minimum: Have several working flashlights with extra bulbs and batteries.

b) Adequate: Purchase at least one flashlight designed for reliability during emergencies. Choose a shake-up flashlight that never needs bulbs or batteries, a wind-up flashlight with long-life LED bulbs, or an LED flashlight that is very bright yet uses a fraction of the battery power of a regular flashlight.

c) Ideal: In addition to flashlights, have candles or kerosene lamps for every room and stairway in your home.

4. Radio

a) Minimum: Have a portable radio with extra batteries.

b) Adequate: Purchase a wind-up or solar powered radio, which will not run out of power for an extended emergency.

c) Ideal: Purchase handheld, person-to-person family radios for better communication between family members.

5. Shelter

a) Minimum: Have tarp and twine in your survival pack to make a makeshift shelter. Store sleeping bags if you live in a cold climate

b) Adequate: Purchase a lightweight backpacking tent in case you need to leave your home. Store sleeping bags if you live in a cold climate.

c) Ideal: Purchase a larger tent and store for emergencies that require you to abandon your house but not your area or if you evacuate in your car. Store sleeping bags or warm blankets. If you don't have a tent, store tarps or plastic, rope and tape to make an emergency shelter.

6. First Aid

a) Minimum: Have a first aid kit and first aid book on hand (available from any drugstore).

b) Adequate: Add items to your basic kit, such as ace bandages, butterfly bandages, and burn gel. Prepare to survive for a longer stretch without medical help.

c) Ideal: Besides a complete first aid kit, purchase a copy of *Where There Is No Doctor,* which provides thorough coverage of medical emergencies. Get first aid training or first responder training and volunteer in a local emergency services program to get experience.

7. Medicine

a) Minimum: Obtain a one-week supply of family essentials.

b) Adequate: Store a one-month supply. Freeze or refrigerate – ask your pharmacist.

c) Ideal: Store a three-month supply. Freeze or refrigerate – ask your pharmacist.

8. Temperature Control

There is no easy fix for heating or cooling houses when there is no electricity. The first step is to look at your most pressing needs, heat or air-conditioning and get creative in finding non-electric solutions to make sure your home is livable no matter what time of year a disaster strikes.

For keeping warm:

a) Minimum: Store long underwear, warm socks and hats, sweaters, sweatshirts and coats, thin gloves (so you can still do things with the gloves on). Also store extra blankets or sleeping bags.

b) Adequate: Purchase a stand-alone, un-vented kerosene heater (must have adequate ventilation).

c) Ideal: Install a wood stove, if your circumstances permit. Some people have a wood stove (set up to vent out of a window) in storage to use only in case of an emergency. Obtain a two-week wood supply.

For keeping cool:

Purchase solar-powered fans. Wet neckerchiefs and drape them around your neck and wrists. Wear lightweight clothes. Wear a hat in the sun.

9. Important Papers

Keep all your important papers (bank account information, titles to cars and houses, insurance papers, credit card information, birth certificates, social security number) in one place. Have a *copy* of all important papers in one envelope outside the house, or stored with your emergency survival gear.

10. If You Have to Leave Your Home

a) Put together a daypack with all the items you would need if you had to evacuate your house (water, food, light, radio, warm clothes).

b) Purchase a 72-hour backpack that contains the essential items. Add clothes and personal items. Include sleeping gear and a tent. Include your personalized first aid kit and medicine, your important papers, and the other emergency gear you've prepared.

c) Have a 72-hour backpack for each member of your family and one for the car.

Note: A checklist for a 72-hour backpack can be found on page 96.

CHAPTER 3
Natural Disaster Scenario

The Davidson Family

The earth shook. Even though it was five in the morning and Tom had been sound asleep, he knew immediately what was happening. He sat upright in bed, listening to the windows vibrate so violently he couldn't believe they weren't breaking. He could feel the bed sway beneath him and watched as the one favorite picture they had on their bedroom wall came crashing to the floor. Jeanne, Tom's wife, was also wide-awake but seemed to be deriving some feeling of comfort and safety from remaining under the covers. The Big One had finally come.

The shaking seemed to go on for the longest time but in fact it was actually less than 30 seconds. Then, utter silence and darkness. No read-out on the alarm clock, no night light in the hallway.

When his head cleared, Tom sprang out of bed. He thought about his children. At exactly that instant, screams came from down the hall. Tom fumbled around the nightstand for his flashlight. Then he and Jeanne hurried down the hall. Opening the door they saw that the smallest boy had been thrown from his toddler bed and lay in the middle of the bare floor, crying. The top bunk bed had been shaken off its posts and had crashed down, pinning the occupant of the lower bunk beneath it but, fortunately, not squashing him. The occupant of the top bunk also lay in the middle of the floor.

The teenage boy and girl, each in their own rooms, seemed to have fared a little better except for the shards of shattered glass that littered their beds and floors from broken mirrors, pictures and bottle collections. After locating slippers or shoes for everyone's feet to protect against the broken glass that seemed to be everywhere, they all congregated on the king-sized bed in the parent's room.

With everyone safe and accounted for, Tom began to assess the situation. The house was still standing. From the incredibly cold influx of air that was permeating the room, he figured there must be a number of broken windows somewhere. The electricity was off. With an ever so slight feeling of relief, Tom realized that the preparations their family had spent so much time and energy on over the last several months were going to pay off.

Jeanne lit the kerosene lamps as Tom hurried downstairs to check out the rest of the house. He noticed a distinct smell of gas so he decided to turn off the natural gas with the special tool he had bought for this purpose. It would be light in an hour or so and then everything would be easier to deal with.

The Watson Family

In another house, exactly the same distance from the epicenter of the earthquake, another family was jolted awake as the shaking began. Joe and his wife Karen started their day in a way very similar to Tom and Jeanne. As soon as the shaking stopped, Joe fumbled down the long hallway in the pitch dark to the laundry room where he last remembered seeing a flashlight. "Ouch," he yelled as he cut his hand on some broken glass. He had to put pressure on the cut for quite some time to stop the bleeding before he could resume searching for the flashlight. When he finally found it, the light was so dim it was virtually useless. He dared not even stop for a bandage but quickly ran back to check on his three children before the flashlight gave out.

Everyone was safe with only minor cuts from broken glass. However, the task of finding shoes for the children was difficult in the dim light. Finally the youngest child had to be picked up and carried as the flashlight flickered and then gave out.

It was unclear where to gather since every room was dark and cold. They finally sat in the living room. Even though Karen had been successful at gathering up blankets and quilts to put around the children, they all grumbled and complained. It was cold and they lived in an all-electric house. Even with the coming of daylight soon, there was not a whole lot to look forward to.

The Davidson Family

The wood fire was roaring and several kerosene lights had been lit when Jeanne and the kids finally came downstairs an hour later. Tom was busy taping large pieces of cardboard over broken windows. A pot of hot water was starting to boil on top of the wood stove. The Davidsons had lived with wood heat for over 12 years so this was nothing new. The woodbin was full and there were two cords of wood neatly stacked just off the back porch. At least they would all stay warm.

The day progressed without too much trouble and by the time dinner was over, everyone was pretty tired. They all retired early. The only damper on the success of the day was the worry for their friends and relatives in other parts of the city.

Over the past several months the Davidsons had been motivated to prepare for an emergency. They had been meaning to do it for years and finally there seemed to be so many uncertainties in the world and so many potential disasters that it just seemed stupid not to do something. One Saturday they sat down and started to make a list of things to do and put them in order of priority. "We just took the first thing on the list and focused on that," Jeanne remembered describing to a friend. "When the first thing was accomplished, we turned to the second."

Their main goal had been to begin to secure a degree of self-sufficiency in the basic necessities—water, food, heat, and light. If the electricity went off, they would still have access to these basic necessities. Preparing brought another benefit: Tom and Jeanne found they were no longer as stressed-out about the future. That in itself was worth the effort.

The Watson Family

"Why did this have to happen in the middle of winter?" Joe asked himself. "When are they going to get the electricity back on?"

At first the novelty of wrapping up in blankets and quilts had occupied the kids. But now everyone was chilled to the bone. They had warded off the bitter cold this morning by cleaning up the house. But by mid-afternoon, Joe's back was stiff, his fingers and toes numb, and his spirits depressed.

He could tell by looking at everyone else that they felt the same. The children's constant complaining made him painfully aware of this fact. Joe had considered buying a stand-alone, un-vented heater from the local hardware store last month when they were on sale for just this sort of emergency but he had not quite gotten around to it.

The family had managed to get through breakfast on cold cereal and lunch on sandwiches but he knew everyone would need something warm to eat or drink very soon.

Besides not having heat or a way to cook, the Watsons didn't have any water. The milk, juice and pop were running low already. There was an abundance of snow outside but they had no way to melt it. There was the water in the hot water heater, but when that was gone, what then? How about the water in the toilet tanks?

The one thing the Watson family did have was a battery-operated radio. Joe needed it to listen to his favorite teams when he was away from the house. Now they were able to tune into the emergency channel.

"Stay in your homes. Keep off the streets," warned the authoritative voice. "We have things under control. The Red Cross is organizing emergency shelters in various parts of the city."

The aftershocks were still dangerous, so Joe could understand the reason for the warnings. But practically speaking, the cold was making their home virtually unlivable. But where could they go?

"What was taking the authorities so long? We pay our taxes," thought Joe. "You'd think they would have their emergency plans all in order so that when something happened, people wouldn't have to wait so long."

The Davidson Family

This morning was anything but normal. Two neighborhood families, both good friends, had shown up yesterday evening, cold, distraught and a little sheepish.

"Sorry to barge in on you this way. We just didn't think it would really happen."

"That's okay. Nobody can survive a winter here without heat."

I'm sure glad we have a big house, Tom mused to himself, good-naturedly. Even though the number of people had now nearly tripled, there was an added sense of security in having the friends here. The children sure enjoyed having more kids around.

The Davidsons had spent the previous summer and fall stocking up on as much food as possible. Their pantry was full of canned food and staples. They had simply started buying extra of the non-perishable items that they used each week. Instead of buying two spaghetti sauces each week, they bought three. The freezer was full of meat and bread. Since it was wintertime, it should keep the food frozen for several weeks as long as they kept the door closed as much as possible.

Last year, the Davidsons had bought a gravity flow water filter as a Christmas present to the family. It sure came in handy now. There was a small creek that ran year round through their part of town. They sent the children out to fill up gallon jugs. This water was brought home and poured into the water filter. Pure water came out the bottom spigot of the filter. This provided enough for everyone's drinking and cooking needs.

The Watson Family

This second day was even worse than the first. Last evening they barbecued a hot meal of steak and hot dogs. This used up the last of the lighter fluid and charcoal. The neighbor to the left had a fireplace in his house but no wood. The neighbor four doors down had a fireplace but made it very plain he didn't want any visitors.

The local grocery was no help. Yesterday the owner had shown up and attempted to sell some things even without lights or a working cash register. Joe had always liked him—a really nice guy. However, the people that showed up had their own ideas. Cold, hungry and very scared, their instincts for survival overcame their normal rational thinking. Instead of calmly waiting in line through the tedious process of checking out without computers, people grabbed what they wanted, or rather what they could carry and made a run for it. Word got out quickly and within an hour, every single item on the shelves was gone. The store was completely empty. Rumor had it that all the other stores carrying food, soap and toilet paper had met with a similar fate. When the owners tried to lock the doors, people broke the glass.

It was amazing to think how spoiled his whole family was with all of today's modern conveniences. None of them had ever gone in for camping or any of that outdoorsy stuff. Not having a four-course meal with dessert and their favorite drinks was considered roughing it. Putting together any kind of a meal with what they had available was going to be miraculous at this point. Joe wondered why they hadn't stocked up at all on food or water. They had just always taken the local grocery store for granted. They just hadn't counted on anything ever going wrong.

The freeway systems had suffered major damage. It was not a simple fix. Many of the overpasses and bridges in a 100-mile radius had sustained damage and some had collapsed, making travel nearly impossible. There was no way for trucks to get in and the National Guard was having a difficult time getting sufficient food deliveries into the metropolitan areas.

The authorities predicted that it could be as long as four weeks before electricity was restored. It was going to be a long month.

The Davidson Family

It was the third morning after the earthquake and things were starting to fall into a routine. The inconveniences were minor for the most part. The powdered cheese, eggs and milk certainly did not taste like the real thing yet it was surprising what dishes they were learning to make with a little imagination. The physical exertion from all the chores was helping to made everything taste better.

The kids complained because they couldn't play Nintendo. But they were gradually rediscovering the previously abandoned board game cupboard. Games of chess, Clue and Battleship filled the evening hours.

The Watson Family

The floor in the high school gym was really hard. It was actually a relief to wake up and crawl out of your sleeping bag. They had been forced to leave their home two days after the earthquake when they ran out of edible food and when the lack of heat had become unbearable.

They were crowded into the high school gym, the makeshift emergency shelter for the area. One small generator ran a few lights. A large propane tank ran a propane heater. It kept the place tolerably warm.

National Guard units brought small amounts of food each morning but there was just not enough to go around and more people were coming all the time. The voices of small children complaining of hunger and thirst could be heard in all parts of the gym. Outhouses had been set up outside but they had gotten filled up halfway through the second day and apparently there was no way to empty them. There never had been any toilet paper.

Oh, for a hot shower with soap and shampoo!

Someone in the shelter had a handcrank radio. It was hard to say whether or not the advantage of hearing news about the rest of the state outweighed the despair that came from knowing all the gory details. Rioting, sickness from contaminated water, and inadequate hospital facilities were widespread.

For Joe it was hard to imagine they had been reduced to living like this. He had always prided himself on being a good provider for his family. To see his children going hungry was heartbreaking. Where had he gone wrong? When would he be able to make it right again?

The Davidson Family

The day had started out fairly normal. It was nice to have everyone at home and not have to worry about running off to a job. Thoughts about earning a living and paying the bills were temporarily on hold. True, there were some major inconveniences with not being able to run to the store. Fortunately, Jeanne had stocked up on toilet paper, laundry soap and shampoo as well as catsup, oil, and their favorite breakfast cereal. They always bought grains and other staples in bulk. But they had to do without butter, sour cream for the potatoes, maple syrup for the pancakes, dog food, batteries, and toothpaste. But all in all, they knew they were extremely fortunate.

As they sat around the dinner table it was obvious that everyone realized they were especially fortunate that day. One of their friend's children had cut himself seriously when he slipped on some ice on his way to get water. It was a head wound and the bleeding was profuse. Tom had applied pressure to slow down the bleeding while one of the other children ran to their next door neighbor, Richard, who was an EMT.

Richard knew exactly what to do. It took quite some time to get the bleeding to stop and the boy needed oxygen. In the end they decided not to take him to the hospital. They had radio communication with the hospital staff and found out that they were completely backed up with more serious cases. The boy was doing quite well at this point.

They were all grateful for the minimal degree of self-sufficiency their family had achieved over the past few months. There were undoubtedly lots of people who were not going to be so fortunate.

CHAPTER 4
Natural Disasters

Mother Nature is unpredictable. We can all remember sporting events that were rained out, or camping trips where the tent almost blew away. Mother Nature can't be expected to deliver perfect 70-degree sunny weather day after day, all year long. This is reason enough for having back-up food, water, and other supplies.

In recent years the planet has experienced numerous severe natural disasters. There have been earthquakes, tsunamis, hurricanes, tornados, mudslides, flooding, fires, severe winter storms, volcanoes, and blackouts. None of the people affected by these calamities knew weeks in advance that the disaster would hit. Advance warning was limited to perhaps a day, a few hours, or no warning at all.

No matter where you live, there is a potential for a natural disaster. The coastal areas, the plains, the mountain regions; all are susceptible. No one is exempt.

Preparing means that you gather what you need at a convenient time. You buy food, a water filter, and other supplies when there are no shortages. Your 72-hour survival kit is packed so that if a natural disaster is pending you have the best chance of getting out of the way without getting stuck in a traffic jam.

Most of us are guilty of the following types of unproductive thinking:

- "It won't happen here!"

- "We've always had electricity in our house and food on the store shelves, so what's there to worry about?"

- "The government will take care of us. Isn't that what we pay our taxes for?"

It is increasingly clear that:

- It can happen here!

- The flow of electricity and food into our area is not guaranteed.

- The government cannot possibly take care of us, nor do they promise to.

Red Cross President Marsha Evans has said, "What concerns me is the lack of reasonable preparedness on the part of the general public. [Many] Americans are wholly unprepared for a disaster of any description. They have not stocked emergency supplies.... Wake up, America."

The purpose of this chapter is not to teach you about natural disasters. You can learn about them on the evening news. We could elaborate on the potential for the big earthquake in California or the great pole shift or what will happen when the ice caps melt. We could go on for a hundred pages telling heart-wrenching natural disaster stories. However, we don't want to waste your precious time. Time may be short.

What we do want to do is encourage you to start your preparations today. We did it. So can you. We hope our efforts will make it easier for you to prepare for a potential natural disaster.

CHAPTER 5

Water

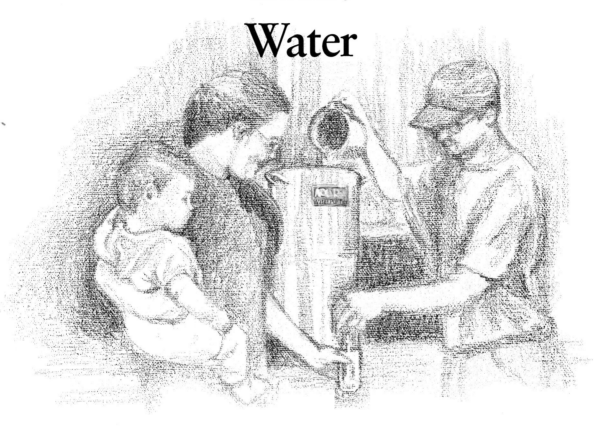

The need for an adequate supply of pure water is second only to the need for air. In the event of natural or man-made disasters, more civilians eventually perish from the effects of bad water than from the direct effects of the disaster itself. This is due to disaster-related breakdowns of municipal water and sewer systems that result in polluted surface water and poor sanitation. Out of necessity, civilians are forced into drinking contaminated surface water. In serious disasters, people need ways to purify the surface water.

Risks to our water supply are constant. Municipal water systems are not good enough, even when all systems are working. A good purification and filtration system is a valuable asset to your daily health as well as a plan for any potential disaster.

In this country we enjoy an abundant water supply that we often take for granted. All we have to do is open the faucet. Disruptions to our supply of safe water have been caused by earthquakes, tornados, droughts, floods, power outages, nuclear power accidents, disease outbreaks and winter storms. These disruptions have lasted from a few days to a few weeks.

Municipal sewer and water treatment plants are dependent on electrical power. Any prolonged electrical power disruption could produce serious water shortages and poor sanitation, due to nonfunctional sewer systems.

Hurricane Mitch, which hit Honduras in November of 1998, knocked out the municipal water systems and drinkable water was in short supply. Hospitals had no running water and sanitary conditions were so bad that doctors canceled all but urgent surgeries. The rivers were contaminated with corpses and chemical pollution—people who bathed or washed clothes in the river started getting skin infections. Doctors in Honduras were concerned about the potential of cholera, dengue fever and gastroenteritis epidemics due to people drinking the polluted surface water.

Even without a disaster, municipal water systems can become contaminated. Most municipal water systems normally contain small quantities of the bacteria Giardia and Cryptosporidium. Usually, humans are not affected by small quantities of these bacteria. Rivers and lakes provide the source of water for water treatment plants in most major cities. Consequently, from time to time, water with higher concentrations of human or animal waste finds its way into municipal water treatment plants. Filtration and chlorine does *not* remove or kill higher concentrations of bacteria.

Giardia is becoming more and more resistant to chlorine, and Cryptosporidium is completely resistant. The only way a public water treatment facility can tell they are having a Giardia or Cryptosporidium problem is when the people drinking the water start getting sick. At this point, the municipal water treatment plant issues a boil water directive. In 1993, an outbreak of Cryptosporidium cyst in the Milwaukee, Wisconsin city water system forced 4,000 people to seek medical attention and resulted in 100 deaths. Since 1965, municipal water systems in the U.S. have experienced over 80 outbreaks of Giardia affecting more than 20,000 people. In Sydney, Australia, three million people were affected. People understand that something is wrong—the use of bottled water has been increasing by 25 percent a year.

Having the equipment and know-how to purify surface water would be essential in the event of a disaster. A person can live about 40 days without food, but only three days without water. A person can lose all reserve carbohydrate and fat, and about 50 percent of the body's protein without being in real danger. A loss of only 10 to 22 percent body weight as water can be fatal. The amount of water lost from the body through urine, water vapor from the lungs, and perspiration averages 2.5 quarts per day.

The effects of dehydration are potentially serious. Symptoms include thirst, sleepiness, apathy, nausea, emotional instability, labored breathing, dizziness, delirium—and finally death. Infants, children, the elderly and physically ill persons are particularly susceptible to dehydration.

Minimum Daily Water Intake

The adjacent chart shows the minimum amount of water required per person per day. The amount varies according to a person's activity level and the temperature. Most experts recommend storing *at least* one gallon per person per day. The average American uses 25–50 gallons per day, which includes the use of washing machines, toilets, etc. One gallon would allow about a half gallon for drinking and another half gallon for cooking and washing. Plan your water storage carefully.

Daily Minimal Water Intake (Person at Rest)	
Gallons	**Degrees Fahrenheit**
.3	60°
.5	70°
.9	80°
1.3	90°

Water Purification and Filtration

There are a number of ways to purify water. These include boiling, chemical purification, activated carbon filters, reverse osmosis (RO), ultraviolet sterilization (UV), distillation and of course, access to a well. Utilize a system that works without electricity: chemical purification, boiling, a hand operated or passive form of activated carbon filtration and wells with hand pumps are the only viable options.

No one water purification system is sufficient to achieve complete purification. Unpurified water can contain four potential health risks: bacteria, viruses, chemicals and heavy metals. A combination of systems is usually required to remove all four.

Boiling

Harmful organisms cannot survive a temperature of 212 degrees Fahrenheit. Bringing water to a rolling boil and letting it remain there for one minute at sea level kills bacteria, viruses, and parasites. At higher altitudes water boils at a lower temperature, so at higher altitudes plan on boiling water for a few minutes longer.

Chemical Purification

Liquid Chlorine

The liquid chlorine method is simple and inexpensive, but it leaves an odor in the water and it does not remove sediment or chemicals. Liquid chlorine is the most commonly used commercial water purification chemical. It kills microorganisms. CAUTION: Do not use granular forms of household chlorine bleach for water purification! Granular chlorine bleach is poisonous! Liquid chlorine bleach is readily available everywhere. Use two drops in a quart of water for purification. Check the date on the bottle because bleach loses strength over time. If it is more than one year old, double the amount. If older than two years, do not use.

Iodine

Another chemical option is iodine, either as a liquid tincture or tablet. For clear water use three drops of tincture of iodine per quart. If the water is cloudy, double the chemical amount. Liquid iodine water disinfectants are highly concentrated and they are not affected by age, air or temperature.

The tablet form of iodine is called tetraglycine hydroperiodide. One brand name for these tablets is "Potable Aqua" and they can be purchased from Yellowstone Trading as well as from many sporting goods stores. Another product variation, "Potable Aqua Plus," comes with ascorbic acid neutralizing tablets that remove the iodine taste from the water. Iodine water purification tablets have a shelf life of two plus years as long as they are kept dry.

Both iodine and chlorine need to be stirred into the water and allowed to sit for at least twenty minutes. If the water is extremely cold or dirty, or if you suspect the possibility of virus contamination, allow the water to be treated for at least forty minutes before drinking or running it through a filter.

Prolonged use of both bleach and iodine can result in health problems.

Activated Carbon

Activated carbon filter systems (ACF) work by passing water through treated carbon. Chemicals, sand and particles stick to the surface of the treated carbon. ACF is the most common type of water treatment. ACF is effective against some chemicals including pesticides, solvents and chlorine, but does not remove heavy metals. There are many different brands of portable filters available.

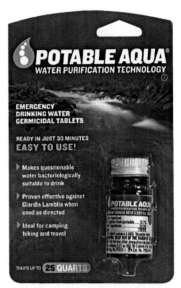

Potable Aqua tablets can make the difference between health and illness.

When selecting an activated carbon filter, a two-stage filter system with 0.1 to 0.3 micron filtering capacity is adequate. A pre-filter removes suspended particles, sand, rust and solids. The second filter removes the bacteria. Water is forced through a filter made of porous material. This porous material has "pores" that only allow particles of equal or smaller size to pass through. The filter media filters out organisms that are bigger than their pore size, like parasites, Giardia, amoebas, Cryptosporidia, and organic material. Many filters have pore sizes small enough to filter out bacteria. The larger pore-sized filters may be fine for use in mountain streams where Giardia is the primary concern, but are not safe for treating water that may have bacterial contamination (for instance, from sewage).

The pore size of portable hand operated filters is not small enough to filter out viruses. In general, viruses do not exist by themselves in water. They are usually found in clusters around organic material. Most filters do a good job of removing organic material and consequently, most viruses. Some water filter manufacturers make a filter that is impregnated with an

U.S. Marines field units use MSR portable water filters.

iodine resin. The idea here is that the silver-coated elements kill viruses as they pass through the filter and deter bacterial growth on the filter element. The only problem with this technique is that under normal conditions, water is pumped through the filter too fast to be sterilized by the iodine resin. Thus some filter manufacturers such as Mountain Safety Research have decided against making a silver resin-coated filter element because it gives the illusion of protection. The best solution is to treat water with iodine for 20 to 30 minutes and then filter the water. A filter with a carbon element will remove chemicals including iodine from the water.

Filters with smaller filter pore sizes take out smaller contaminates and produce cleaner water, but they also become clogged sooner. If the water is very dirty, pre-filter the water with a coarse filter, like coffee filter paper, before running the water through the portable water filter.

There are a good number of water filter manufacturers. These include PUR, Katadyn, First-Need, MSR and Sweetwater. Katadyn is imported from Switzerland and it has the greatest name recognition. Katadyn also costs the most (about twice as much as a comparable MSR unit). The MSR WaterWorks is made in the U.S. It filters to 0.2 microns. The Katadyn unit filters down to 0.2 microns. Katadyn claims the maximum gallons of water filtered before the filter has to be changed (although some manufacturers question their test results). The Sweetwater Guardian filters down to 0.2 microns and it has an optional iodine resin cartridge. The First Need Deluxe filters down to 0.4 microns. The PUR Hiker filters down to 0.5 microns. The PUR Explorer/Scout and Traveler models filter down to 1.0 micron and they also have the iodine resin option.

After doing considerable research on water filters, we decided to carry the MSR water filters at Yellowstone Trading. MSR makes two models: the MSR WaterWorks II and the MiniWorks. Both have a ceramic filter with an activated carbon core that can be cleaned and reused up to 40 times. The WaterWorks II comes with the special PES Membrane. The use of the PES Membrane on the WaterWorks II increases pollutant removal to .2 microns, ensures the removal of narrow profile leptospirosix bacteria and produces pharmaceutical grade water. The U.S. Marines selected the MSR MiniWorks (which filters to .3 microns) for its amphibious operations and reconnaissance missions.

One MSR filter will produce 50 to 250 gallons of purified water depending on the concentration of pollutants in the untreated water before the inner filter element needs to be replaced. The MSR filter will remove disease-causing bacterial microorganisms and chemicals.

Purification cups and straws will filter out harmful bacteria. The water filtration capacity of these units is limited.

Gravity Operated Activated Carbon Water Filters

These filter systems are a good household solution. Gravity water filters are very convenient in that they do not need water pressure to function. The unit is set on a counter, untreated water is poured in the top and gravity forces the water down through the filter.

The AquaRain water filter is the gravity water filter we carry at Yellowstone Trading and it is one of our best-selling products. It produces safe drinking water with natural water pressure, using no electrical energy or chemical additives. The filter elements remove waterborne pathogens including cysts and bacteria. It utilizes the tightest effective filtration available, providing purified water that far exceeds EPA standards. The activated carbon core absorbs pesticides, organic chemicals, chlorine, tastes and odors. An AquaRain unit is in use in the Washington, D.C. EPA office!

AquaRain gravity water filter

An AquaRain gravity water filter provides unlimited fresh drinking water from almost any water source.

The Aqua Rain is simple to use. Even your children can filter water and they will probably enjoy doing so. It is also very effective in producing large quantities of pure water. It will produce 25–30 gallons of water per day. This will not only supply your family's needs for water but will produce an abundance of good drinking water that you may want to share with your relatives and friends.

One of the comments we hear the most from our satisfied AquaRain customers is how good the water tastes.

Reverse Osmosis

Reverse osmosis is a natural process that uses pressure to force water through a semi-permeable membrane, from a more concentrated to a more dilute solution. This membrane has microscopic openings that are smaller than viruses and bacteria. RO removes viruses, bacteria, parasites, salt, heavy metals, and heavy-molecule chemicals. RO does not sterilize the water. For this reason RO units should be used in conjunction with a UV system to ensure sterilization. An activated carbon filter should also be used in conjunction with an RO unit if there is a concern about chemicals in the water. Most RO units will not work without AC current and substantial quantities of water.

Ultraviolet

Ultraviolet light is used for purification at water bottling plants, breweries and dairies. Hospitals also use ultraviolet light for disinfection. Ultraviolet water purification systems kill viruses and bacteria that filters don't remove without the use of heat or chemicals. There are three basic wavelengths of ultraviolet light and only one is of value in purifying water, UV-C 100–280 nanometers. This light is invisible to the human eye. This wavelength is 99.98 percent effective in killing viruses, algae and bacteria. This is also referred to as germicidal radiation. An ultraviolet lamp radiates invisible light into the water; when the proper micro-wattage is delivered it will kill microorganisms.

The Steri-Pen is a pocket-sized, handheld, battery-powered, ultraviolet water purification system. The Steri-Pen disinfects 12 ounces of water in 30 seconds simply by stirring. It is rechargeable and can perform 30 treatments per charge.

The PURA UV1 is a non-portable high technology flow-through device that uses ultraviolet light for purifying water. It needs electrical power to function, but it may work for those with good generator systems.

Other Sources of Pure Water

Wells

Nothing beats a good well with a hand pump. It is low-tech and it generally produces good water—unless the well is polluted to start with, too deep to pump by hand, or overly mineralized.

Well water is first filtered by the earth. The quality of well water varies greatly from property to property. It costs about $15 to $25 to have well water tested by the local Department of Health.

Hand-pumps provide emergency water insurance during electrical disruptions.

Hand-powered well pumps that will move water 250 feet can be purchased from Lehman's Non Electric Catalog. These pumps are expensive. Shallower well pumps that reach to a depth of 75 feet can be purchased at a lesser cost. Wells more than 250 feet deep will require an electrical pump, either AC or DC, and, of course, electricity. See the power generation chapter for more information.

Rainwater

Rain is a drinkable water source. Gather it in clean containers before it touches any other surface. It should be considered contaminated after contact with the ground or a dirty surface. Rainwater should not be used without purification if there is any evidence or concern that biological, radioactive, or chemical agents have been dispersed in the area.

Solar Still

Solar stills are fairly easy to construct. Instructions can be found in any wilderness survival book.

Storing Your Water

Water storage presents several challenges. If water is stored outside the home, it must be placed where it cannot freeze.

Solar Still

Tube to Suck Water Out

Hole In Ground

Water Collection Container

Plastic Sheeting

Dirt

Water From Condensation

Add the makings of a solar still to your 72-hour survival kit: six feet of plastic tubing, a six by six plastic sheet, and a water container.

The second problem is preventing bacterial growth. Adding one teaspoon of liquid chlorine bleach for every five gallons of water will prevent the growth of algae and bacteria. The water tank or containers should be emptied and re-filled with fresh re-chlorinated water at least once every six months.

The third challenge is storage space. At 1.25 gallons daily, four people need five gallons per day. That means 14 five-gallon containers constitutes a two-week supply: enough to fill most of the kitchen. That's why water purification is a good option if you have access to a water source. (See the end of this chapter for ideas on additional water sources.)

Water is heavy. One gallon of water weighs eight pounds.

Shelf Life of Water

The shelf life of water is difficult to determine. It depends on several factors, including the original quality of the water, the temperature at which it is stored, and the amount of exposure to light. Stored water should be inspected at least every six months. Check for changes in appearance, taste and odor as well as leakage. Manufactured bottled water often has a shelf life date that can be checked. Label and date water just as you would your food.

If water simply tastes flat, it can be aerated by pouring the water back and forth from one container to another three or four times.

Maintain maximum shelf life by storing water in the dark. Containers can be covered with dark plastic bags or a tarp. It should be stored away from gasoline, kerosene, paint, pesticides or chemicals, as fumes can penetrate any plastic container and contaminate the water.

Types of Water Containers

Like food, water should be stored in food-grade containers and in a cool, dark area. Food-grade plastic containers are available in 5-, 15-, 30- and 55-gallon sizes. Plastic water tanks and concrete water cisterns hold large volumes. Used containers present the risk that the water will taste like whatever was stored in the container previously. If you decide to go with used containers, clean them first. Use a solution of 1/8 teaspoon chlorine bleach mixed with a gallon of hot water. Do not use soap. After using the bleach solution, rinse the container thoroughly with plain water.

Glass jugs and bottles will not retain odors, if cleaned thoroughly, but have the disadvantage of being breakable and much heavier.

Mylar water bags are plastic bags that look like aluminum foil on the outside. They hold five gallons, have a built-in plastic spout and fit into a cardboard box sold with the bag. The boxes can be stacked three high. Other plastic bags could also be used if they are food-grade plastic. Most other bags are treated with insecticides and pesticides.

Plastic barrels and drums are made to hold and dispense water and some are made to withstand outdoor freezing temperatures. Otherwise, leave room for the water to expand if it freezes.

Additional Water Sources

Consider all sources of water in an emergency. Remember that a source of water is only as good as the water is pure. Make sure that any source of water you use is made safe to drink.

1. Hot water tank

Immediately after a major disaster, you can prevent contamination of the hot water tank supply by shutting off the water valve that leads from the water main into the house. The tank can be drained if it remains upright. You must first turn off the gas or electric supply to the tank and close the water intake valve (the faucet at the top of the tank). Drain water into a container by opening the faucet at the bottom of the tank. Never turn the gas or electricity back on until the valve is reopened and the tank is full of water.

2. Water remaining in the pipes

If your home is multilevel, you can drain the existing water in the pipes by gravity flow, after the water line into the house has been shut off. Open a faucet on the top floor and drain water from a faucet at the lowest level.

3. Water dipped from the flush tank (not the bowl) of the toilet.

Must be purified before using. Do not use "blue" or chemically treated water.

4. Water from a swimming pool.

Do not drink without filtering with a filter equipped to remove chlorine (such as the AquaRain).

5. Water beds.

Some waterbeds contain toxic chemicals. If you designate a waterbed in your home as an emergency water source, drain it yearly and refill with fresh water containing two ounces of bleach per 120 gallons. Or use the water for hygiene purposes only.

Note: To learn about water and radioactive contamination, see the Appendix.

CHAPTER 6
Food

Most Americans take food and the farmer for granted. No longer attached to the land, we are out of touch with the rhythms of nature, away from personal participation in the annual cycle. It used to be that most people had gardens, planting in the spring, tending during the summer, harvesting in the fall, and putting up food for the winter. This change represents a very brief exception in the long span of human history.

The current norm of cheap and abundant food requires no real participation on the consumer's part. Since the public has not experienced a food shortage in recent history, they tend to take the welfare of the nation's farmers for granted. But a combination of bad weather and a changing economy has caused thousands of farmers to go under in the last several decades. Most food is no longer grown locally. What makes things even worse is that a lot of the food Americans eat today comes from outside of the U.S. This puts most of us in a vulnerable situation.

Any prolonged power disruption would lead to a telecommunications breakdown and disruptions in electronic commerce. A nuclear or biological attack upon the United States would disrupt the food production and distribution network, resulting in a nationwide food shortage.

Prepared people will be able to take care of themselves and will be able to help others. The coming years may result in a return to a more balanced way of life, but may also include natural disasters, disrupted weather patterns with attendant crop failures, and political and social upheaval. This may bring out the best qualities of self-sacrifice in many persons who rise to the challenge of the times; far-sighted people will do their best to prepare.

How Much Food Do Supermarkets Really Have?

Under normal circumstances, the modern just-in-time warehousing system provides the consumer with an incredible variety of foods at bargain prices. But the average supermarket only has three to four days worth of food in stock.

A survey of supermarket managers concluded that the general public never purchases food more than a few hours ahead of an expected emergency. Most people wait until the last minute, even if they have received advance warning. They start shopping when the snow starts falling, when the hurricane is less than half-a-day away, or when the river is starting to overflow its banks.

A few hours before the storm hits, the general public rushes in and buys what they think they need: primarily bread and water. This is referred to as panic buying and is quite different from making preparations.

The infrastructure for the production and distribution of food is much more vulnerable than most people think, and very technology-dependent. Getting the food from the field to the table involves a lot more than going out in the field and picking vegetables. Most major crops are shipped by rail to food-processing facilities. The railroad system is computer dependent.

Why Stock Up?

In the case of a nationwide food shortage, local communities would be in a desperate struggle to feed themselves. A government study undertaken back in the 1970s determined that far more Americans would die from starvation in the year following a nuclear attack than would die from the bombing.

Prepared people are not dependent people. In the event of a disaster they aren't a burden on strained and inadequate government relief efforts. People stocking up when there is abundance helps the farmers and the economy. More important, in the event that a real shortage occurs, the fact that some people have stocked up will mean that fewer people will have to compete for the limited available supplies.

The importance of food becomes more apparent when you start totaling the quantity used over a year's time. The average American eats over 1,400 pounds of food a year! This breaks down to about:

- 370 pounds of fruits and vegetables

- 140 pounds of cereals

- 240 pounds of meat and fish

- 350 pounds of dairy products

- 350 pounds of other items

Preparation is not just saving food. Buckets and cans eventually empty, so consider renewable food options if at all possible. Put away a quantity of non-hybrid garden seeds. Experiment with sprouting. If you live in a rural area, raise animals like chickens and goats. Not only will you have your own meat, eggs and milk, you will have extra food to barter with.

A long-term food storage program should meet the specific needs of you and your family. Use the guidelines in this chapter to determine what kind of program you need. Get started now and don't forget the can opener!

Stocking Up

We recommend that every family have a four-month food reserve. In addition to a long-term food program, you can begin stocking up so that you are prepared with food for a few days or more in the event of a weather disaster, power outage, tight budget, or even unexpected extra company. Although these tips are not a substitute for worst-case scenario preparations, they are keys to getting started. Try to anticipate all potential food ingredients needed, because in a disaster, you probably won't have access to a grocery store.

1. Start stocking up on foods that your family likes to eat regularly. Put a sheet of paper up on the refrigerator door and keep track of everything you use for a two-week period. This will give you a basis to compute how much of what items you use and project how much you'll want to buy.

2. With each shopping trip, gradually build your reserve food stock. Ready-to-eat items are important such as canned meats or fish, dried fruit, nut butters and dry cereals. Buy one or two extra of each item canned or packed in airtight packages. Don't heavily stock up on items with a limited shelf life; remember which items need to be rotated yearly. When you get home, label your cans and packages with the purchase date. Rotate your stock so you are always using the oldest and keeping the newest. Set up an inventory system so that items are replaced as they are used up.

3. Stock up on paper goods: paper plates, trash bags, paper towels, wet wipes, toilet paper, diapers and feminine supplies.

4. Try to buy at the best prices possible. Get together with friends and neighbors to order case lots and bulk items.

5. Store items carefully and in sealed containers if they are not already packaged. You will need sealed plastic buckets, tote containers or smaller new galvanized garbage cans with tight-fitting lids as protection from moisture, insects or mice. If containers are not food-grade, store food inside the container in a food-grade plastic bag. See the "How to

Store Your Food" section later in this chapter for more information on containers.

6. A long-term storage program will benefit from specially processed survival foods. Supplement your pantry with freeze-dried or air-dried foods, MREs, and powdered milk and eggs.

7. The best long-term storage option is a pre-made low-moisture food program that will get you through any scenario. These programs come in various configurations, volumes and price ranges. Their major advantage is that they are low-moisture, come packed in larger #10 cans, and the oxygen is removed from the can. These factors facilitate the longest possible shelf life. Their cost per-meal is comparable to supermarket food.

Planning a Food Program – Bottom Up!

When designing your food storage program start from the bottom up instead of the top down. By bottom up we mean to look at what your family likes to eat and try to approximate this in your program.

Top down designing is when you shop for a generic one-year food supply without any consideration of how you are going to use it. Introducing new strange foods to your family in times of crisis might make you pretty unpopular. Plan ahead now for "camping out" and enjoying it.

Obviously, shelf storage life is a challenge, but this can be met by continually rotating, consuming and replenishing items in your food storage program that have a shorter shelf life. Examples are mayonnaise, canned tomatoes, ketchup, pickles, and spaghetti sauce.

Purchase a good food storage cookbook. (Cookbook sources are listed at the end of this section.) Use the cookbook plus your family's favorite recipes to put together a rotating 30-day menu plan.

Calculate the quantities of each item needed to fulfill the menu for the full 30 days, including spices, leavens, oil and sweeteners. Then multiply the totals times the number of month's worth of food you want to have. Then BUY THE FOOD!

Nutritional Guidelines

Considerable research has been undertaken in recent years to develop guidelines and recommendations for food storage programs. Yellowstone Trading has put together a four-month and a one-year food package that provide a comprehensive, nutritionally balanced program consisting of a broad variety of dehydrated fruits, vegetables, proteins, grains, seeds and legumes. These programs provide a hearty diet for a normally active adult for the allotted time period.

Most people don't have enough variety in their storage programs. Some of the older conventional food storage programs consisted of four basic food items: wheat, powdered milk, honey and salt. Wheat can be considered a backbone of an inexpensive storage program because of its long shelf life, nutritional balance and utility. Properly stored, wheat lasts virtually forever. Three Forks, Montana wheat is the best wheat on the planet. It has something to do with weather conditions, moisture, temperature and possibly even altitude. All wheat is rated on how it compares to wheat grown there. This hard red wheat makes the best flour for whole wheat bread.

However, research suggests that some people can't survive very well on a diet in which whole wheat is the main staple. Many people are allergic to wheat and don't realize it because they are only consuming a small amount of whole wheat in their daily diet. They can tolerate refined wheat products (made with unbleached or white flour), but not whole wheat products. But once whole wheat becomes a major staple in their diet, they experience complications. This is especially true with young children.

One solution is to purchase less wheat and substitute a variety of whole grains, including quinoa (pronounced keenwah), amaranth, spelt (a cousin of wheat) and kamut (an ancestor of wheat). Quinoa and amaranth have virtually no gluten and may be tolerated by those who cannot eat wheat. Although both spelt and kamut have gluten, people with wheat allergies more easily tolerate them.

Kamut was used in ancient Egypt. Kamut has 20 to 40 percent more protein than modern wheat, and makes excellent pastry, noodles, cereals and baked goods.

Spelt was the staff-of-life in early Europe. Its de-husked kernels were consumed as a whole grain staple food, gaining spelt the reputation as "the rice of Europe." After nourishing Europe's Golden Ages, spelt almost completely vanished. It has been re-discovered recently growing high up on the mountainsides of the Alps. Spelt is the ancestor to modern wheat. It has a highly water-soluble fiber that dissolves easily for efficient nutrient assimilation. Spelt is richly supplied with nutrients, has a hearty nut-like flavor and is delicious used for baked goods, cereals, pastas, breads and flour.

Quinoa is indigenous to South America and this grain-like food has been cultivated in the Andes since at least 3000 B.C. It was the mainstay of the Inca culture. Quinoa is high in protein, calcium and iron and is now grown in Colorado. Quinoa has a 15- to 20-year storage life when properly packaged in an oxygen-free environment. It can be cooked and served like rice or added to baked goods.

Amaranth comes from the Aztecs and from China. It is a member of the pigweed family and is grown at lower altitudes than quinoa. Amaranth is rather tricky to cultivate but the tiny grains produce flour used in making breads, cereal and pasta. Amaranth can also be cooked like rice. The grain has a strong, slightly bitter flavor.

A balance of beans and grains can add both flavor and variety. They are inexpensive and together can provide complete proteins.

Appetite Fatigue

Some food storage programs have insufficient variety, resulting in appetite fatigue when people get tired of eating the same foods every day, and at times they will prefer not to eat at all. Children are especially susceptible to this phenomenon. One way to make your program more appetizing is to add some instant soups and sauces, dehydrated fruits and vegetables, and freeze-dried meats. This can turn a very limited diet into a tasty menu.

Vitamins and Minerals

Vitamin C, D and multivitamins are important supplements to a long-term storage diet. This is an especially important consideration for children since their bodies don't store reserves of nutrients like adults' do. Vitamins are particularly needed during emergencies, as stress depletes vitamins and minerals and is a major contributor to sickness and disease.

Vitamins may lose their potency, but they can be stored and rotated into daily use. Also, digestive supplements are a must! Most dehydrated food is difficult to digest.

Calories

Calories and protein content are important components of any food program. According to the American Red Cross, the average male adult uses up to 3,000 calories and 70 grams of protein a day. Packages that only supply 900 to1200 calories per day could be a starvation diet. Look at the quality of the calories and protein. Does the food package get the bulk of its calories from white sugar and does it contain inexpensive soy-based protein? The better programs contain honey and real freeze-dried meat.

Comfort Foods

Some foods are psychologically comforting. Good food is critical to the morale of your family. The single most important factor affecting a person's physical and mental health during a crisis is the quality of the food available. They say that the best food program is to store what you eat and eat what you store.

Imagine the comfort of being able to serve and eat familiar, tasty food during an emergency.

Even the Office of Civil Defense recommends that you select familiar foods, saying they are heartening and more acceptable during times of stress. Try Jell-O, puddings, tapioca and the makings of a pie. It may seem frivolous but they can help normalize an otherwise drab diet and take the attention off the grains and beans. Carla Emery, well-known author in the self-sufficiency field, names desserts and sweets first.

It is hard to make radical dietary changes overnight, especially for children. In some cases children have been known to starve rather than to eat unfamiliar food. So store jam and peanut butter to keep the kids from starving and make sure your program includes familiar condiments, herbs, spices and seasonings.

If your children are used to drinking milk, they might find the taste of nonfat powdered milk disagreeable. One alternative is a whey-based milk drink. It tastes good and is loaded with vitamins and minerals. It can be substituted for milk in recipes. This product is available through Yellowstone Trading.

Plan Ahead

Prearranging and practicing your survival procedures, including food preparation, will allow for continuity of normal life and your ability to direct your attention to the most critical tasks at hand.

Collect the recipes you like the best and have them handy. Be prepared to make what your family likes. A crisis situation does not lend itself to the cook trying out new recipes.

Have all the ingredients for your first week of emergency cooking laid out ahead of time. Try out some of the meals in advance. Plan a weekend cookout for family and friends. Last of all (or first of all), don't forget a good can opener and a bucket opener for 5-gallon pails.

Condiments, Oils, Seasonings and Spices

Include in your food storage program sufficient quantities of flavorings such as bouillon, onion, garlic, your favorite herbs, soy sauce, chili powder, mustard powder and, of course, salt and pepper. Ingredients needed for baking include: baking soda and powder, active dry yeast, powdered eggs and milk, cinnamon, vanilla, honey and other sweeteners.

Honey and sugar have always been items of high barter value during food shortages. In addition, honey has a medical history of being curative and being effective in treating wounds, infections and burns.

Stock enough cooking oil. In Europe shortly after World War II, people were familiar with hunger. One quart of vegetable oil was a highly prized commodity because of its scarcity, flavor and high caloric content.

Recent research on oil and fats has determined that the kind of fats and oils we cook with and eat is as important as the amount. Fat intake should be moderately low, between 20 to 30 percent of total calories. Monosaturated fats are considered heart-healthy. One storable source is olive oil. When purchasing olive oil, select either virgin or pure grades. Any other grades are chemically extracted. The pure grade of olive oil can be used in almost all recipes. Extra-light olive oil or a vegetable oil should be chosen for baking. Sesame oil is another healthy oil that stores well. Canola oil also stores fairly well, but recent studies have indicated possible negative side effects from prolonged use. Try to find oils that are expeller pressed and avoid hydrogenated oils.

MREs (Meals Ready to Eat)

MREs or meals ready to eat were originally developed for the military. They are fully hydrated and precooked meals with an individual portion vacuum-sealed in a foil laminate. Drop the foil laminate packages in boiling water to heat or eat cold. MREs are especially valuable for grab and run emergency packs and situations where cooking and meal preparation are not feasible.

MREs last for about three years. They are loaded with sodium. Plan on drinking lots of water with them. Autopsies of soldiers in Viet Nam who

Apple Almond Crisp, an AlpineAire breakfast entrée, would be a welcome break from oatmeal every morning. Enjoy tasty emergency food when rotating your supply.

subsisted on MREs for extended periods of time indicated that the high sodium content could contribute to serious health problems. They should not be relied on for extended periods of time, but they do have their place.

Freeze-Dried Entrées

Consider supplementing your food program with freeze-dried meals. AlpineAire offers a variety of tasty freeze-dried entrées that come in either #10 cans (gallon size) or foil pouches. The foil pouch option makes these entrées very lightweight and compact. Another advantage is that they require little or no cooking. They are prepared by adding hot or cold water and can be eaten in many cases "as is." Because they are preserved without water, they weigh

AlpineAire lightweight food pouches are ideal for on-the-go emergencies, while storage in #10 cans enables an extended shelf life. Most items last 8–10 years under proper storage conditions.

less then other comparably nutritious foods. These characteristics make AlpineAire entrées very useful in a disaster scenario where a person has to make an emergency relocation and is limited in what he or she can carry. AlpineAire pouch entrées are very popular with backpackers. Rumor has it that the Navy Seals prefer AlpineAire freeze-dried meals to MREs.

AlpineAire meals don't have quite as long a shelf life as plain grains and beans (some may last up to eight years). But they are very tasty and easy to rotate into your daily diet. AlpineAire entrées include 31 vegetable, seafood, chicken, turkey and beef meals, 14 side dishes, ten desserts, and three soups, so there is a lot to choose from. Unlike MREs, these entrées are not loaded with sodium, preservatives and white sugar. They are very healthy. Contact Yellowstone Trading for more information on no-cook, freeze-dried foods.

There are numerous energy bars and emergency food ration bars on the market as well. They cannot be viewed as a long-term nutritional food source, but could be stocked in the trunk of your car or for emergency situations where you have no other source of a quick energy boost.

In spite of all the innovations in food preserving and long-term storage, we unfortunately still have not seen the development of the freeze-dried pizza.

Renewable Food Sources

Self-Sufficiency Gardening, Livestock and Hunting

We are personally not too optimistic about the idea of living out of #10 cans and 5-gallon buckets. Above and beyond appetite considerations, they are not renewable food sources. As renewable food sources, gardens and small livestock can be a valuable addition to your preparedness plans.

Baby goats are cute and an adult milking goat could be an invaluable resource during an extended food shortage.

It's a great idea to grow your own garden and/or a community garden every year and get in the habit of canning fruits and vegetables. A vegetable grown from a non-hybrid seed will produce seeds that can be planted and will yield vegetables the next year, enabling you to grow and save your own seeds.

Stockpile a good supply of canning lids, rings, jars and vinegar, and several years' worth of non-hybrid garden seeds.

Goats can pretty much live off the land. They can live eating the bark off trees. You may not get the highest production and flavor of milk under these conditions, but goats will survive when the cow has died for a lack of hay. Consider other renewable food sources such as sheep, chickens, rabbits, turkeys and bees as part of your long-term food program.

Read more about self-sufficiency in *The Encyclopedia of Country Living* by Carla Emery. It is a wonderfully complete resource guide for everything you might want to know on these subjects. It is available through Yellowstone Trading.

During the Great Depression in the 1930s many people managed to stay alive and feed their families

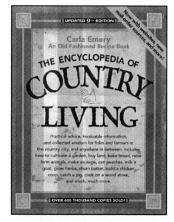

Encyclopedia of Country Living **is a single-source resource providing the knowledge of our rural ancestors. If you didn't grow up on a farm you need this book!**

with wild game. Most Americans don't know how to gut an animal, let alone track one down and shoot it. Hunting is a skill and it takes time and experience to become proficient. If you have time and access, develop hunting skills. What may be recreation now could be a matter of survival in the future.

Sprouting

Storing seeds and beans for sprouting is a great idea. Most of the food in your storage program is effectively dead. It will supply you with carbohydrates, protein and sugar, but it is devoid of enzymes and vitamins. Sprouting is easy. Sprouts can be grown almost anywhere. They are packed with vitamins, minerals and proteins, live enzymes and fiber. Sprouts are also a source of antioxidants. They're a concentrated resource, as one-third cup of seeds will yield over a pound of fresh sprouted greens for a cost of 25 to 30 cents.

Sprouted seeds and beans provide live food, vitamins, and enzymes as part of a food storage program.

Choose from a large variety of seeds and beans: alfalfa, broccoli, cauliflower, red clover, kale, mung beans, mustard, onion, radish and wheat.

Seeds store best in non-permeable plastic, each different kind separately, in a cool, dry, dark place. Store extra water for sprouting. If you haven't tried sprouting before, now is a good time to start.

Live Food Supplements

There are numerous products on the health food market that feature dry powdered greens that, mixed with water or juice, provide a highly nutritious drink. These include green kamut and green barley. Powdered greens can be combined with other powdered grains and vegetables to produce a dry "superfood" drink mix. These highly concentrated powders provide an excellent addition to your storage program.

Dehydrating

Consider dehydrating some of your own foods. Dehydrators help preserve fruits, vegetables, and even meats. Home-dehydrated foods can be stored in Ziploc bags or vacuum-sealed jars. Home-dehydrated food is not as low moisture as commercially dehydrated food and will not have as long a shelf life.

Cookbooks for Food Storage

Just Add Water, by Barbara G. Salsbury

Cooking with Home Storage, by Vicki Tate

Making the Best of Basics, by James Stevens

How to Store Your Food

The cooler the storage environment, the longer the storage life of the food. Food stored in areas exposed to summer heat and temperature extremes will degenerate rapidly. Food stored in living areas of your home will be warmer than food stored in a cool, dark part of the house.

Identification of food containers is important. Contents and the date of packaging should be clearly marked. If more than one party is sharing storage space, the owner's name should be on each box, can or bucket.

Be organized! Place food into storage according to a workable plan. If the cook can't find the food, what good is it? Whatever the emergency, food can be one of the most comforting and normalizing elements for everyone. The cook is one of the most important people in the community and must be given all assistance possible to prepare satisfying meals.

This means a kitchen and storage area intelligently planned out, accessible food, an accurate inventory, a pre-planned menu, and reasonable privacy for the cook to work in. Post a map in the kitchen showing where the food is stored, so that if more than one person is cooking, everything is findable.

Packaging and Containers

Food packaging and storage is an integral part of the program. Food needs to be protected from oxidation, moisture, rodents and insects—possibly for years. This can only be accomplished if the food is properly packaged for long-term storage.

Not re-packaging your grains and beans is a formula for disaster. People who have stored food in their basements or garages in burlap, plastic or paper bags or in cardboard boxes have usually regretted their decision. We have seen numerous instances of mice infesting food storage areas.

Another potential problem is ground water seeping into underground storage areas. Do not underestimate the amount of moisture in the ground! Direct contact with water causes paper bags to rupture and spill, and then grains will mold, rot or ferment. If moisture finds its way into the storage area, it will raise the humidity, soften the paper bags, and begin to spoil the unprotected food. Ripped bags and spilled grain are a certainty when damp or weakened bags get moved around.

Containers need to be manageable. Most people can handle a 5-gallon plastic bucket full of grain, or a case of six metal #10 cans, but find a 6-gallon bucket a bit too heavy. Shape is important because it relates to the efficient use of precious storage space.

The 5-gallon rectangular metal tin is by far the most efficient container. It allows nearly 100 percent of available storage space to be utilized because it has no taper or rounded edges. A 5-gallon rounded plastic bucket wastes almost 40 percent of that available space. The tins are, however, more difficult to handle than buckets because they don't have handles. Cases of #10 cans are nearly as space-efficient as the rectangular tins.

As the designer of your food storage program, you may choose the containers you prefer. However, there is no perfect food storage container. The perfect container would be airtight, easy to open and close, hard as steel, rustproof, stack nicely in use, and nest within itself when not in use. It would also be inexpensive, have a comfortable carrying handle, come in several sizes and finally, be rectangular and without a taper for space efficiency. Short of perfection, one should choose the most practical container based on the circumstances at hand. Following is a brief comparison of plastic buckets, metal tins and metal #10 ($3/4$ gallon) cans.

Plastic 5-Gallon Buckets

The plastic round buckets are the least expensive choice; they don't rust and they come in two standard sizes, 5 and 6 gallon. They are easy to carry, commonly available, and will nest when empty. Plastic buckets stack fairly well up to three or four buckets high, depending on the weight of their ingredients. They are 95 percent rodent proof (in some extreme instances, rats and ground squirrels have gnawed through the sides of buckets). Plastic buckets tend to be hard to open and the lids may be damaged when the bucket is opened without a bucket opener tool. Due to their shape, round buckets tend to waste storage space. They also cost more to ship.

Metal 5-Gallon Rectangular Tins

Metal 5-gallon rectangular tins store the most food in the least space. They are airtight, rodent-proof, stack well in block, and easy to open. But these containers are more expensive, harder to carry, harder to find, dent easily, come in only one size, are subject to rusting, and they won't nest when empty.

Pictured is the user-friendly #10 can.

#10 Metal Cans

The #10 metal can holds $3/4$ of a gallon and is the easiest container size to handle. This container is fairly space-efficient and because of its small size is the best container for dehydrated fruits and vegetables. The #10 metal can is the most airtight long-term food storage container. Cases are cardboard boxes that hold six cans and stack beautifully. It is the best size for kitchen use and allows vacuum packaging. This container is the most expensive option. It also requires a mechanical can closer to crimp the lid on the can. This makes it a little harder for do-it-yourself canning.

55-Gallon Steel Drums

Beekeepers use a variation of a 55-gallon steel drum that has a removable top lid and a food grade interior coating for storing honey. These drums cost from $12.50 to $20 each. They are particularly handy for storing large volumes of wheat and beans. The downside of these containers is they are hard to move and transport when full. Locate the nearest commercial beekeeper and if he doesn't have any spare ones to sell, he can put you onto a source for these barrels.

Protection and Preservation of Contents

Most long-term storage foods have a moisture content of 10 percent or less. This is sufficient to prevent mold growth. These dry foods will tend to pick up additional moisture from the air, which will decrease their stability (shelf life). A major goal of packaging for storage, then, is to keep the dry foods dry. Suitable moisture-resistant containers accomplish this.

A second challenge is to prevent rodent damage and insect invasion. Since a determined rodent can gnaw through plastic, metal containers are best for extended storage. (However, we have successfully stored an abundance of food in plastic buckets for extended periods of time.)

To control insects, first procure grains and seeds that have been cleaned to USDA standards for No. 1 grain. This will greatly reduce but may not eliminate infestation already present.

To completely control insects in food requires fumigation by the inert gases of nitrogen or carbon dioxide. Whenever the oxygen in the container is flushed out by one of these gases, the living insects inside will smother from lack of oxygen. Carbon dioxide, unlike nitrogen, is also toxic to insects if present in high enough concentration.

Another solution to the bug problem is to add bay leaves. Five dry bay leaves in a 6-gallon bucket of grains or beans will prevent insect infestation —apparently the bugs just don't like them.

Mylar Bags

Keeping food in a vacuum helps preserve it. But all plastic breathes a small amount. Over time, minor amounts of air migrate through the walls of a plastic bucket. A Mylar plastic bag liner greatly reduces this gas transmission. These bags are very strong. They are 4 mil thick, have an outer layer of aluminum and three additional inner layers of plastic. In general, they are opaque, airtight and waterproof and when properly sealed, they will hold a partial vacuum.

This is important if oxygen absorber packets are being used to remove the oxygen from the inside of the plastic bucket. Oxygen absorber packets create a partial vacuum in the container. Using oxygen absorber packets without a Mylar plastic bag tends to cause the sides of the bucket to suck in, especially at altitudes over 3500 feet. Many buckets are not strong enough to hold this vacuum and deform. The Mylar bag liner eliminates this problem by containing the partial vacuum to the inside of the bag.

Using Mylar bag bucket liners increases the labor involved in putting food in a bucket. Once filled with the ingredient and the two 750 cc. oxygen absorber packets, the end of the Mylar bag has to be heat-sealed before the bucket lid is hammered on. The temperature of the bag sealing iron needs to be adjusted so that the end of the bag is properly heat-sealed. If this is done right, the seam cannot be pulled apart without destroying the bag. If the temperature of the iron is set too high, it will destroy the strength of the bag, and if it is too cool, the seam can be pulled apart fairly easily.

When attempting to seal the Mylar bag liner, place a 20-inch 2" x 4" board on one side of the bucket. Fold or pull the end of the bag over the 2" x 4" and heat-seal the bag by ironing the bag against the board with a conventional clothes iron.

Not all foods warrant this added preparation. If you are putting food away with the goal of using it within the next five years and if the ingredients are mainly beans and wheat, all of this extra Mylar bag work might not be a very big issue. Wheat and beans are fairly stable.

Oxygen Absorber Packets

Oxygen absorber packets are the newest innovation for eliminating oxygen inside of long-term food storage containers. Oxygen absorber packets are a desiccant, like the packets found in vitamin and prescription bottles. These packets come in two sizes, 450 cc. and 750 cc. One 450 cc. packet per #10 can will absorb the oxygen once the can is closed. Two 750 cc. packets are used for a 5- or 6-gallon plastic bucket. These are only to be used with dry ingredients and not with oil, honey or other liquids. The beauty of oxygen absorber packets is production speed. Packaging food, be it by hand or machine, is much, much faster with oxygen absorber packets compared to nitrogen or CO_2.

Nitrogen Packing

Very few canning operations still use nitrogen because using oxygen absobers greatly speeds up production. Nitrogen flushing controls insects and eliminates oxidation. Insects are smothered because oxygen is removed from the container and replaced by nitrogen, an inert gas. Preservation is accomplished because with the removal of oxygen, oxidation ceases. Oxidation is a chemical reaction involving oxygen that causes food to loose flavor, color and nutritional value.

True nitrogen packing is a three-stage process. The first stage is to draw a vacuum on the container and remove the air. Next, the container is flushed with nitrogen gas, removing the vacuum; and finally the container is hermetically sealed. Thus, the air has been replaced by nitrogen, and no vacuum remains within the food container.

The second variation of nitrogen packing involves flushing the container without first vacuuming out the air. This method is not as effective since it only replaces a portion of the oxygen in the container, but it has its place in some instances and is better than no treatment at all.

Another option for packing is to draw a vacuum on a container (usually a canning jar) and hold the vacuum while the container is sealed. No nitrogen is added. This process does remove the oxygen, and will be effective as long as the vacuum is maintained. While sometimes useful for household food preservation, this method is not used by storage food suppliers.

CO_2 Flushing

Many storage food items keep well with a minimum of treatment. Most grain and beans are stable and will keep their nutritional value for years if kept cool and dry. They are, however, prone to harbor insects, such as weevils and moths. The use of carbon dioxide, in a simple process called "CO_2 flushing" or "CO_2 packing" will very effectively eliminate these pests.

The principle here is not the elimination of oxygen, but elevating the levels of CO_2 in the storage container. Slightly higher-than-normal CO_2 levels will kill insects, rodents, and incidentally people (if they are in a sealed environment). Simple equipment is used, consisting of a bottle of pressurized CO_2, and a regulator, hose, and injection wand. The cans or tins are filled with the food product and a specified volume of gas is injected into the container before it is sealed.

Unfortunately, plastic buckets cannot be flushed with CO_2. While nitrogen is inert and non-reactive (one of the "noble gases"), CO_2 is not. It reacts over time with the interior walls of the plastic bucket, chemically bonding with them. In doing so, the gas vacates the spaces around the food product inside the bucket, and in fact will cause a powerful vacuum to be created inside the bucket. This wouldn't be so bad, except that it causes the buckets to "suck in" from the vacuum effect. This distortion can weaken the bucket's stacking ability, and often is so severe that the walls crack, admitting air and insects.

Diatomaceous Earth

There is an additional way to control insects in stored grains and beans, the simplest of all methods: adding Diatomaceous Earth.

Diatomaceous Earth (DE) is a marine deposit that is mined from the earth, ground up into a fine, talc-like consistency, and used by many farmers to prevent insect infestations in silo-stored grain. Microscopic marine creatures called diatoms formed these deposits millions of years ago. The silica shells of diatoms are extremely abrasive to insects, scratching off the protective waxy coating on their shells, thereby killing the insects from dehydration.

DE works as well in buckets as it does in grain silos and is completely non-toxic to humans and animals. Favored by natural farmers over chemical fumigation of silos, it is an inexpensive method for those packaging their own food. Few commercial suppliers of storage foods are aware of DE and none are selling products treated with it.

Freeze-Drying vs. Air-Drying

Freeze-drying is a process in which a raw or cooked food item is flash-frozen, then placed in a vacuum chamber in which the moisture in the food is drawn off. This is a sophisticated method that relatively few processors have the equipment to accomplish. It is a super way to preserve food, but the products are more expensive than air-dried foods. Some dried foods are only available in freeze-dried form, including meats.

Freeze-dried foods cook much faster than air-dried. Freeze-dried green peas, for example, need only boiling water poured over them and they are ready to eat in about five minutes. Air-dried peas must be cooked in boiling water for about 20 minutes. That's a lot more cooking fuel!

Air-dried dehydrated foods are less expensive than freeze-dried. Air-drying causes the foods to shrink, making it possible to put more food in a can. Hence, air-dried foods take less storage space—as much as 75 percent for some items. Air-drying is something that one can do oneself.

Frequently Asked Questions

1. How long will dehydrated food store if I do not open the can?

The chart on the accompanying page outlines basic guidelines for life expectancy of basic food ingredients, but the question is not an easy one to answer. It depends on how the food was packaged and the conditions under which it is being stored. Very little scientific testing has been done to determine shelf life. With minimal care, a storage life of five years can be expected for 95 percent of storage foods.

Ideal storage is in a dry area that can be maintained at about 40 degrees. Since this is impossible for most of us, 50 to 70 degrees is acceptable, but will result in a shorter shelf life. Any higher temperatures will rapidly decrease the shelf life of your food stores. Good locations are along north walls, close to the floor, in root cellars, in basements without heaters, or even under the house, if it is always dry.

Some foods are more sensitive than others. Dehydrated oily products

Food Storage Life Expectancy

Description	Nutritive Storage Life	Storage Life Before Spoilage
Grains and Beans	Indefinitely	Indefinitely
Rice, Brown	1–2 years	Not good for storage
Rice, White	3–5 years	Approx. 3 years
Sprouting Seeds	10 years +	Indefinitely
Powdered milk, low-fat	5 years	Indefinitely
Honey	Indefinitely	Indefinitely
Baker's Yeast	1–2 years	5 years with refrigeration
Powdered Butter	2–3 years	5 years with refrigeration
Garden Seeds	3–5 years	10 years +
Salt	Indefinitely	Indefinitely
Freeze-Dried Foods	7–15 years	Up to 15 years
Dehydrated Foods	7 years	Up to 15 years
Herbs Capsulated	3 years +	Indefinitely
Vitamin C	2 years	10 years
Olive Oil	Indefinitely	Indefinitely
Commercially Canned	6 months – 1 year	Up to 3 years

Note: The one factor that has the greatest effect on the longevity of food in storage is a cool, stable, temperature. Food subjected to the fluctuations of summer heat and winter cold will degenerate quickly.

Nutritive Storage Life = The length of time a particular food can be stored and still retain most of its original nutrients.

Storage Life Before Spoilage = The length of time food can be stored before it spoils and thus becomes dangerous to eat.

have a shorter shelf life. These include butter and margarine powders, cheese powder and to a lesser degree, powdered milk. These may need to be replaced after just a few years. If liquid vegetable oils are stored, they should be checked for rancidity after one year. Monounsaturated oils with high oleic acid content, like olive oil and canola oil, have a naturally higher resistance to rancidity than other oils.

2. How long will the food keep after I have opened the can?

Freeze-dried foods (meats, fruits or vegetables) can be stored for up to three months, if care is taken to always keep a plastic lid on, and if the can is stored in a cool, dry place. Other low-moisture foods should have a minimum storage after opening of four months, possibly more.

3. What equipment do I need?

1. The can opener and bucket opener

2. Grain mills

Invest in a good handmill, if possible. Since the bulk of most long-term food programs is made up of grain, it is very important to have some sort of non-electric means of turning grain into flour and meal. Yellowstone Trading offers a choice of two different hand-powered grain mills.

3. Pressure Cooker

Pressure cookers cook faster, use less energy and are one of the best ways to re-hydrate dehydrated foods. Pressure-cooked foods retain more nutrients.

The Country Living Grain Mill lasts a lifetime, transforming bulk grains into nutritious foods for just pennies a meal.

The Worst-Case Scenario

Rationing, Hiding and Hoarding

People who stock up ahead of time, when there is no shortage, are not hoarders. People who wait till the last minute and then try to strip the store shelves of food might be considered hoarders.

Today, most people who are serious about storing emergency food have had to make sacrifices in other areas in order to budget for this purchase. They have made the decision to spend their money on a food reserve just as they would any other asset.

The USDA previously maintained strategic grain reserves to feed the American population in the event of a national emergency, but these reserves for the most part have been liquidated. Much of these wheat reserves were sold to the USSR. In 1977 the Soviet government completed a five-year food storage project that provides their entire population with two pounds of grain per person per day for 300 days.

Access

Most of your food storage should be kept in a discrete, temperature-stable location. Two to four weeks worth of food should be immediately accessible.

Choose an adequate storage site based on the actual amount of cubic storage space required. A basic one-year, one person, low-moisture long-term food supply requires about 21 cubic feet of storage space. This would equate to an area approximately 3 feet high by 3 feet wide by 2.5 feet deep. An entire family's one-year food storage would easily fit into a corner of a basement. Canned food that is not dehydrated will require a larger storage space.

To learn about food and radioactive contamination, see the Appendix.

CHAPTER 7

Heating and Cooling
Cooking and Refrigeration

After water and food, heat could be your most critical survival factor. Modern life depends on electricity, which can be interrupted by natural disasters, extreme weather conditions, or nuclear war. Electricity affects our ability to both heat our homes and cook our food.

A winter emergency could be the most difficult to address. Of course, there are portions of this country where heating is not a necessity. But for most of us, heating is a must in the winter. A house with no heat could be completely unlivable. One man who went through Canadian ice storms remarked how the cold greatly affected his family both emotionally and physically.

Heating

Without electricity, even natural gas and propane furnaces won't work. Furnaces require electricity for the functioning of the blower and burner assembly.

A wood stove is a good solution to both heating and cooking challenges. Wood stoves come in many sizes and styles with a wide price range. Cooking is possible on stoves with flat tops, and some will even heat your hot tub! If you can't heat with wood on a normal basis, you can purchase a wood stove with an emergency window installation kit and keep it in storage until needed.

Airtight stoves are the most efficient but are not an absolute necessity. Look for a stove that is designed for radiant heat efficiency without an electric blower. Most pellet stoves require electricity to feed the pellets so do not rely on these stoves.

The Riley stove offers many advantages. It has a flat top for cooking, an oven built around the stovepipe and two 5-gallon hot water tanks with faucets on the sides. These stoves are reasonably priced, ranging from $139 for the smallest stove to $819 for the largest stove with oven and hot water tanks. Riley Stoves also offers a pellet stove that does not require electricity to work. This may well be the best option for emergency back-up heat. For many people it would be easier to stockpile pellets than firewood.

Some water heaters have a thermo-siphon system, meaning they function with a passive water circulation system and do not require an electrically powered circulation pump. These units are typically used for heating hot tubs. A hot bath once in a while might be very comforting if times get hard, especially in the winter. Riley stoves are available through Yellowstone Trading.

The Riley Stove with large shelf, 4-gallon water tank and spark arrestor.

Unvented Heaters

Another option for heat without electricity is an unvented heater. While these heaters do not require any kind of vent through the ceiling, in a confined area the fumes will build up requiring adequate ventilation—like an open door or window. They can be obtained in kerosene, natural gas or propane versions. Harbor Freight sells household natural gas and propane radiant heaters. Kerosene heaters are available through camping supply stores. Building codes prohibit or restrict the use of unvented heaters in some areas because they can cause asphyxiation if adequate ventilation is not present.

Cooling

When the electricity goes off, the air conditioners and swamp coolers are not going to work. For most people, this will not be a life-threatening situation. However, for elderly people in very hot climates it would be a good idea to secure a solar-powered fan. These fans would use the energy of the hot sunlight to keep the air moving, and thus lower the temperature.

Unvented heaters require no chimneys or stovepipes; with a supply of fuel they can mean the difference between going to a shelter and staying home.

Here are some additional suggestions for keeping cool. Wet neckerchiefs and drape them around your neck and wrists. Wear lightweight clothes. Wear a hat in the sun.

Cooking

A wood stove solves the cooking challenge. However, any standard propane cooking stove will probably still work during any emergency. These stoves do not use up much propane. Keep the tank full in case of an emergency.

A camp stove works as long as the fuel holds out—so stock up. Options include Bunsen burners, Cook 'n' Heat ethanol in a can, butane stoves, propane stoves, Coleman stoves, etc.

Solar Cookers

Solar cookers focus the sun's rays onto a cooking chamber. The fuel is inexhaustible as long as the sun is shining! Sun Toys makes an inexpensive and very portable unit. It folds to a 14" x 14" x 2" packet and bakes at temperatures up to 300 degrees F. The Global Sun Oven is more sub-

The Global Sun Oven bakes, boils, steams, or roasts food with energy from the sun.

stantial and cooks at a higher temperature, 360 degrees F. It weighs 21 pounds and it folds into a small 19" x 19" suitcase-sized package. The Global Sun Oven is used daily in 126 countries around the world. These solar cookers can also be used to melt snow and purify water. Both are available through Yellowstone Trading.

Refrigeration

It is not practical to try to power a conventional refrigerator during a disaster with a generator or a low-voltage energy system. The generator would have to run all day long in order to power the refrigerator. In a disaster that causes an extended loss of power, refrigeration may not be needed, since there probably won't be any food available at the local grocery store. Eating dehydrated or canned food: chances are there won't be too many leftovers.

The only real need for refrigeration will be to store meat from a freshly slaughtered animal, or for milk if you have a goat or cow.

A freezer, on the other hand, is of much more value. It can preserve frozen meat and other products for a long time. In much of the world people have to eat an entire animal as soon as it is slaughtered because they don't have refrigeration or freezers.

Refrigerators and freezers are available in both propane and kerosene versions. The propane versions are more user-friendly. The 8.5 cu. ft. Fros Tek propane freezer uses about two gallons of propane per week. Siber makes kerosene refrigerators and freezers. These appliances will need ventilation.

With the use of a generator, a conventional 110-volt freezer will continue to work effectively, provided the door isn't opened often and the generator runs once in the morning and once at night.

CHAPTER 8
Light

Bright, carefree and inexpensive lighting for every room of the house is a modern luxury, made possible by electricity since the early 1900s. Very few of us have any idea what it might be like to live without electric light. We think, "Oh, we'll be fine with a few candles and an old-fashioned kerosene lamp."

To get an accurate picture of what it means to live without electric lights, turn off the fuse switches in your house some dark winter evening. Doing this in advance, when there is no emergency, will give you a far better picture of what you need to do to prepare than reading any number of books on the subject.

Having adequate, safe, non-electric light for every room is highly recommended and achievable. Even with a generator and fuel, you may have electricity for just two hours each morning and evening. At other times it's wise to use alternative lighting.

Lighting supply list:

- Flashlights, batteries and bulbs
- Kerosene lamps
- Candles

Flashlights

Flashlights will be invaluable any time the electricity is off. Options include:

- Standard flashlight with extra batteries and bulbs
- Standard flashlight with rechargeable batteries, battery charger and bulbs
- Wind-up flashlight
- Flashlight that recharges by shaking

The standard flashlight with regular batteries is the least expensive option. The better the flashlight is made, the more reliable it will be. Be sure to stock up on extra batteries and bulbs.

Every family member needs a flashlight. MiniMag lights are available in pouches that hang from a belt. Standup flashlights, also known as battery-powered lamps, would be another good option.

Rechargeable batteries provide long-term security, provided the battery charger works off the grid. Independent sources include a generator-run electric charger or a solar battery charger. Rechargeable batteries are a good idea, yet they do seem to wear out more quickly than you think they will.

DeWalt and Pelican make high quality rechargeable commercial flashlights. These flashlights feature heavy-duty construction and a convenient unit that detaches from the flashlight and goes into a recharger when the flashlight is not in use. Options include a 12-volt battery charger and a 110-volt charger.

What usually goes wrong with flashlights is that the batteries die or the bulbs break. Wind-up flashlights with LED bulbs solve both problems by combining wind-up technology with the reliability of unbreakable bulbs. These are a great solution to the problem of run-down batteries. We don't know about you, but our regular flashlights always seem to end up with dead batteries when we really need them. But as long as you can crank, you can get light from this type of flashlight. One minute of winding gives one hour of light.

With a wind-up flashlight, power is always available

Standard LED flashlights work with minimal battery use. LED bulbs use about 10 percent of the power of a regular bulb and with two "D" cell batteries, a single bulb LED flashlight should run for about two weeks straight. LED bulbs are virtually unbreakable. The CC Expedition LED flashlight has seven white LED bulbs that will provide a bright cone of light for more than 40 hours on one set of batteries. After 40 hours it does continue to provide useful light for up to several hundred hours. The U.S. military uses a special version of the CC Expedition LED. This flashlight is waterproof up to a depth of 160 ft.

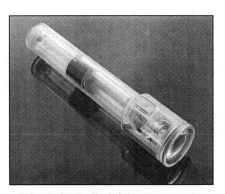

This shake-up flashlight never needs batteries or bulbs.

One other flashlight option is the Night Star LED Flashlight. It recharges simply by shaking it. Electrical energy is stored in a capacitor that powers the flashlight's white-light LED bulb. This flashlight is not extremely bright but is usable and dependable. In a worst-case scenario, with this flashlight you would never be without light. These flashlights are available through Yellowstone Trading.

Batteries for Flashlights and Radios

Conventional Alkaline Batteries

The downside to conventional alkaline batteries is they are not rechargeable. Another problem is that the battery power gradually decreases as the temperature drops and they will not provide adequate electrical power below 0 degrees F. The benefit of the alkaline batteries is low initial purchase cost. However, this does not necessarily mean they are cheaper than other battery options when you prorate the cost over a year's time.

NiCad Batteries

The virtue of NiCad batteries is they are rechargeable. NiCad batteries are ideally suited for low-drain applications where the batteries are charged about three times a year. They will hold a charge for up to six months.

On the downside, NiCad batteries are subject to "memory effect." If a NiCad battery is constantly recharged when half of its electrical capacity is still in the battery then it will eventually start to lose some of its storage capacity. The solution to this problem is to fully discharge the battery once a year. If you have a voltmeter, check the discharged battery to see if it has reduced its charge to 1 volt. This annual discharging process will reduce the damaging "memory" problem.

New NiCad batteries require several charging and discharging cycles before they will produce full power storage and output. New NiCad batteries should be given an initial overnight charge and then the power should be drained from them completely by putting them in a flashlight or some other appliance, turning it on and allowing it to drain the battery. Repeat the process several times. Do not overcharge NiCad batteries. Overcharging will reduce the useful life of the battery. NiCad batteries can be stored indefinitely, but batteries that have been stored for a long period of time should be given the same treatment as "new" batteries (described above).

When recharging NiCad batteries, if you are charging more than one battery at a time and one of the batteries has a lower charge then the rest, the lower charge battery will "sacrifice" itself to the batteries with a higher charge. After a number of charging cycles the weaker battery will "sacrifice" to the point of becoming permanently dead and will no longer take a charge.

In terms of charging NiCad batteries, slower is better! Fast charging will result in shorter battery life.

Nickel Metal Hydride Batteries

Nickel metal hydride batteries provide more power than alkaline batteries. They are rechargeable and they do not have a "memory effect." The useful life of this battery is about 500 charge - discharge cycles. The nickel metal hydride battery is ideal for those who use batteries daily. The downside is that they cost more than NiCad batteries and they have a fairly rapid self-discharge rate. Leave it on the shelf for long and it will be low on charge or dead when you go to use it.

Lithium Batteries

The main advantage of Lithium batteries is that they continue to provide electricity at low temperatures, below 0 degrees F. Another advantage is that it does not self-discharge! They can sit in storage for years and still hold the same charge. The downside to Lithium batteries is that they are not rechargeable and they cost more.

Battery Chargers

There are many types of battery chargers. The Eco-Charger charges both alkaline and NiCad batteries—it's unique because alkaline batteries are not normally rechargeable. It won't restore dead alkaline batteries, but it will bring them back up to charge when they start getting low.

A solar powered recharger works when the electricity is out, and it's also great for

A solar powered charger keeps battery power coming as long as there is sun.

backcountry camping. The better units include a voltage meter to indicate battery charge level, which helps prevent over-charging and diminished battery life. They require about eight hours of sun to fully recharge batteries. Solar-powered battery chargers will recharge nickel cadmium and nickel metal hydride batteries, but not alkaline batteries. Inexpensive solar-powered battery chargers can be purchased from Yellowstone Trading.

Lamps

Lamps that work without electricity are among the most valuable emergency tools. Several varieties run on kerosene (cheap but smelly) or lamp oil (more expensive but cleaner burning).

Kerosene lamps with circular wicks put out enough light for reading and other close work.

Aladdin lamps use a mantel and give off a light bright enough to read by. The glass chimney and the cloth mantel are very fragile. Have extra mantels and chimneys on hand. They come in several models and are more expensive than other kerosene lamps but well worth it.

Regular kerosene lamps provide sufficient light to live by but not for reading or close-up work. For general lighting, order lamps that mount to the wall. With wall-mounted units in each bedroom, bathroom, and stairwell, the whole house is functional without having to worry about lamps getting knocked over.

One style of kerosene lamp can be safely carried around. The glass chimney is securely anchored to the lamp. They are handy for doing chores after dark.

The tabletop model of kerosene lamps is available from your local hardware or discount store. Be extremely careful when moving these around because the glass chimneys are unstable. Purchase extra wicks and chimneys.

A more expensive, durable and versatile alternative to the Aladdin lamp is the Petromax Lantern. It burns lamp oil, kerosene, diesel fuel, and gasoline or aviation fuel. Only lamp oil or kerosene should be used inside a house or confined area because the other fuels give off toxic gases. With either of these two oils, this lamp gives off a bright light and will burn for 12 to 15 hours with a quart of fuel.

Lamp oil or kerosene are available from various sources. If using kerosene, get the #1 grade. Lamp oil is just a cleaner, more refined grade of kerosene.

Coleman lanterns have been used for years to provide lighting for hunting, fishing and camping trips, and to provide illumination for jungle landing strips. Admiral Byrd carried them on his trek to the South Pole and they have been used over the years when natural disasters have knocked out utility power. Coleman lanterns burn "Coleman" fuel or unleaded gasoline. These lanterns should only be used with good ventilation. They give off toxic fumes, but represent a good option for outdoor use. The silk mantles are very delicate once installed on the lanterns—any jiggling or bumping causes them to deteriorate. So stock plenty of spare silk mantles. Coleman lanterns are relatively inexpensive and can be found at any local camping store. Purchase a "dual fuel" model, which will operate on either "Coleman" fuel or unleaded gasoline. The standard models operate only on "Coleman" fuel, which is relatively pricey and might not be readily available during a disaster.

See the Power Generation chapter for information on fuel preservatives for the long-term storage of gasoline and kerosene.

Have a fire extinguisher on hand when using either lamps or candles. Make sure it is fully charged and operational and that every member in the family has been trained to use it. Functioning smoke alarms are a must. Outdoors, buckets or barrels of water are low-tech tools to prevent fires from spreading.

Candles

Candles are a good option for rooms that don't require bright light. Tall taper candles are not recommended because they can be easily knocked over, and the hot wax tends to drip. Candles in glass or metal

holders large enough to catch the melting wax are safest. 36-hour or 120-hour emergency candles are one of your most reliable, yet least expensive options. Don't forget the matches!

Warning: open flames and unwatched flames present extreme fire danger. As a general rule, candles should not be left untended. Even kerosene lamps on stable tables can be knocked over by wind or falling objects.

With this 36-hour candle, use one or more wicks depending on how much light or heat is needed.

CHAPTER 9

Communication

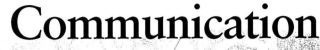

How to Stay in Touch with Family, Friends and Community Before, During and After an Emergency

Did you notice how long it took family members to find each other after Hurricane Katrina? Prior planning can avoid this painful situation. Most of us are so used to the convenience of telephones and cell phones that we take them for granted as a means to staying in touch with our families. But this type of communication is dependent on electricity.

When the power goes out, the communication stops.

Telephones need electricity. An older phone that does not plug into an electrical outlet may work for a while as long as the telephone company has electricity. In a citywide emergency, it is unlikely that the phone company will be able to supply service.

Cell phones will work as long as their charge holds and the cell phone company has electricity to keep transmitting. In a prolonged power outage, the cell phone towers may go off, too.

Radio and TV will not work when the electricity goes out, and the studios may not have power to produce shows.

So what can you do to ensure that your communications will go on uninterrupted? You'll want to connect with family, friends and government agencies. Each may require a separate solution.

Staying in touch will greatly improve the psychological health of everyone involved. The unknown is the result of being cut off from what is going on elsewhere. Speculation lends itself to wild imagination, fear and insecurity. We have all experienced the discomfort of waiting for someone to call or show up. We worry and imagine the worst. This tendency is even greater when real danger threatens.

Do you remember elementary school when the firemen gave a talk on fire safety? You went home with a paper to fill in, showing your home, with instructions to mark two escape routes from every room and the spot outside your home where everyone would meet when you were all safely outside. Having everything planned out ahead of time was the key.

Today, most of us spend the day away from the home and family. Dad works one place, mom another and the children are off at different schools. What if the emergency happens in the middle of the day? Weathercasters may provide hurricane warnings, but earthquakes, fires, and terrorists don't.

What to Do NOW Before an Emergency

1. Sit down with your family and discuss contingency plans. For the children, if possible, suggest a place to meet that is within walking distance, like the library or local market. It would be difficult to determine which place would be safe, so choose more than one. Have places to meet that your children can walk to both from their school and your home.

2. Choose a relative outside of your area that can be a center to receive messages. It is possible that members of a family might end up in different emergency shelters with no way to communicate with each other. All family members agree ahead of time to attempt to get a message to that person about their condition and location as soon as the crisis has subsided. Make sure every family member has this person's number with them in their backpack or wallet. Have it posted clearly at home.

3. If you have children, include the teachers and school administrators in your planning. Let them know what you are trying to accomplish and see what emergency plans they already have set up. How will they attempt to contact you in an emergency? Where will the children stay until the threat is over?

4. Give your contact person the phone number of your local police dispatcher, the Red Cross and your local radio station. This will give your contact person the ability to get information concerning your whereabouts in case of a disaster in your area, according to our local Disaster and Emergency Services office.

5. The Red Cross has created a wonderful solution for the problem of contacting family members during and after a disaster. On their web site they write, "If you have been affected by a disaster, this web site provides a way for you to register yourself as 'safe and well.' From a list of standard messages, you can select those that you want to communicate to your family members, letting them know of your well-being. Concerned family and friends can search the list of those who have registered themselves as 'safe and well.' The results of a successful search will display a loved one's first name, last name, an 'as of date,' and the 'safe and well' messages selected." Make sure all family members are aware of this web site ahead of time. See www.disastersafe.redcross.org.

6. Handheld radios are an ideal way for families to stay in touch. They can be carried in backpacks or purses. The limitations are battery strength and the distance they can communicate. Radio Shack carries Motorola handheld radios that can transmit up to 12 miles if there is

a good line of sight between the radios (about $70 per pair). They work when the phones don't. Even if the family member you are trying to reach is out of range, it may be possible to communicate with someone else who has a radio set to the same channel who could then relay your message. The comfort and peace of mind knowing you have done your best to facilitate communication during an emergency should well offset the expense of acquiring these radios.

7. Every family should have a good battery-operated AM/FM/SW radio with spare batteries. Antennas will probably be necessary to ensure reception. Wind-up/solar-powered radios are the best option for reliable communication. Yellowstone Trading carries two types that will always work in an emergency.

    The radio first and foremost will carry emergency broadcasts put out by the police, government agencies or emergency personnel. With normal communication systems cut off, the only viable source of knowledge about what is happening in other areas—locally, nationally or even internationally—could be a radio. Emergency broadcasts could provide critical information to make good decisions.

8. Set up a community telephone tree. In an extreme disaster, there will be no working telephones. However, in many situations, there is some warning of a potential threat. Lead time, from minutes to hours to days, could allow you to plan and act.

    a. Decide first on how many households you want to include in the neighborhood unit. This could be just ten of your neighbors, (everyone in a one-mile radius) if you are living out in a rural area. It could also be 100 to 200 households if you are in a high-density area. The great thing about a telephone tree is that large numbers of people can be contacted quickly with minimal effort on a few people's part.

    b. Next acquire the contact information for those who want to be included in this telephone tree. If there are twenty houses on a certain block, make a list of the addresses of these houses. Include the names that you know. Make up a one-page flyer letting your neighbors know that you would like to set up a community telephone tree and give them your number to call if they would like to be included. Ask who would be willing to be a call person, someone who would call five people to relay information as needed. Pass out the flyers. Keep track of the contact information as people respond to the flyer.

c. When you have the contact information on everyone in the neighborhood that wants to be involved (cell and work numbers) set up all the names in a tree. If you are the initial contact person for your neighborhood, get five names of people who are willing to call. Assign five people to each of these call persons. Now you can communicate with all twenty households in your neighborhood in a matter of a few minutes. If you want to reach larger numbers, add more levels to the tree. The five people that you call will call five more people who have also agreed to be call persons and they call their four people. 100 households can be reached very quickly.

d. Contact the emergency disaster coordinator in your county. Share your idea about a telephone tree. Ask them if they are willing to contact several key people to start a telephone tree when they receive information about a threat. Even one contact person can start a countywide tree.

e. To extend your neighborhood tree to other neighborhoods consider the following avenues. Place a notice in the local newspaper and put up flyers on community bulletin boards letting others know what you are doing and asking for volunteers from the other neighborhoods. Ask your local radio station to run a free announcement. One volunteer from each neighborhood can set up the tree for their area and be a contact point. Churches and other community organizations could also be resources for getting the larger area of a whole county covered.

Now that you have completed all your preparations, one final piece makes sense. Write out a one-page set of instructions covering the emergency procedures that you have agreed upon. Make a note of where vital things are kept, such as your short wave radio, your 72-hour pack, your family handheld radios and the telephone tree info. Make sure everyone in the household knows where this page of instructions is kept (maybe on the refrigerator or other very convenient place). When a disaster strikes, the brain often gets confused because of the high level of fear and uncertainty. Things that you have prepared for in advance may be temporarily forgotten. Having everything written out ahead of time will ensure the best possible outcome.

What to Do DURING an Emergency

First, take comfort from your preparations—you're way ahead of where you would be otherwise. Although it is impossible to plan on exactly how things might unfold, you can adapt your preparations and plans to fit whatever happens. You can act more clearly during the emergency.

Try not to worry. When some things are out of control you just have to make the best of a difficult situation. A positive attitude will be your greatest tool. Make full use of your preparations and use your radio to gather information.

What to Do AFTER an Emergency

After the most serious threat has abated, remember your communication plans. Contact that relative out of the area. Use the Red Cross web site previously mentioned. Keep your short wave radio on to keep you informed of what the emergency personnel are doing and what they may not be able to do because of being stretched too thin. Use the resources you acquired ahead of the emergency to make your survival more comfortable and to help others.

Basic Radio Technology

Radio communication operates through the use of electromagnetic energy. When electrical power flows through a radio station's antenna, it transmits an electromagnetic radiation in all directions. This electromagnetic broadcast is referred to as a radio wave. Radio waves travel best through outer space and air, but to a lesser extent they transmit through earth and water. The radio communication spectrum includes a wide range of radio frequencies.

The three basic terms that describe radio waves are amplitude, wavelength and frequency.

Radio waves have a crest (high point) and a trough (low point). The strength or amplitude of the radio wave is the distance between the crest and trough.

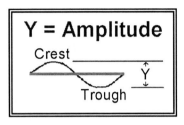

The wavelength is the distance between the crests of the wave. A short wavelength is a radio wave with a short distance between the wave crests and a long wavelength is a radio wave with a long distance between the wave crests.

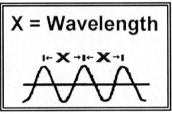

Frequency is the number of complete waves that occur in a given radio wave in one second. A higher frequency radio wave has a shorter wavelength.

Low and high frequency radio waves are measured in kilohertz (KHz), thousands of cycles per second; and very high frequency radio waves, measured in megahertz (MHz), millions of cycles per second.

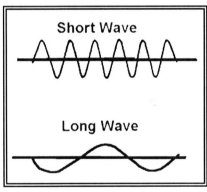

The AM radio band is medium frequency. It starts at 540 KHz and increases to 1600 KHz or 1.6 MHz. AM stands for amplitude modulation and FM stands for frequency modulation. This relates to two different ways of connecting sound with a carrier wave. The FM band is in what is called the very high frequency range (VHF). It starts at 88 MHz and increases to 108 MHz.

AM radio broadcasts long distances but is susceptible to static interference. FM does not have the extended range of AM, but it produces a clearer signal. Lower frequency radio waves transmit their signals further because they bounce off the ionosphere and reflect back to earth, thus enabling them to go over the horizon. Higher frequency radio waves are limited to line-of-sight transmissions.

One advantage to higher frequency is that it penetrates buildings and earth better than lower frequency. For this reason, emergency medical services in many cities use UHF (Ultra High Frequency) instead of VHF.

Receiving

Government controls radio communication in almost every nation in the world. The U.S. government assigns frequencies for certain purposes. Specific bands are allocated for citizen, emergency service, commercial broadcasts, military, cellular, satellite telemetry, marine and amateur.

There are many signal sources that can provide a variety of information. For listen-only mode, an ordinary AM/FM household radio will work, but our recommendation would be to obtain an extended range receiver. This range should be from 155 kilohertz (KHz) to 30 megahertz (MHz) and be capable of detecting signals that are either amplitude modulated (AM), frequency modulated (FM), Single Side Band modulated (SSB —either upper or lower side band) or continuous wave (CW) telegraphy. The receiver usefulness is greatly enhanced when it can receive signals in the very high frequency (VHF) band from 120 MHz to 180 MHz FM. A separate small vertical VHF antenna is desirable for this band.

Commercial AM/FM Broadcasts

While many commercial radio stations will not be operating during some emergencies, the government utilizes commercial stations as part of its emergency broadcast system. Because stations are located over a large

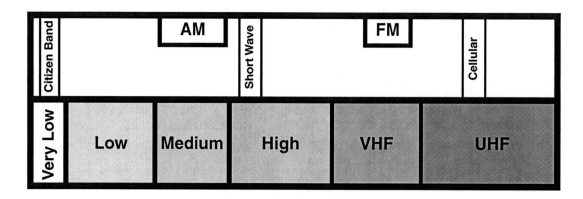

Very Low Frequency	VLF	10 – 30 KHz	30 – 10 Meter
Low Frequency	LF	30 – 300 KHz	10 – 1 Meter
Medium Frequency	MF	300 KHz – 3 MHz	
High Frequency	HF	3 – 30 MHz	Short Wave
Very High Frequency	VHF	30 – 300 MHz	
Ultra High Frequency	UHF	300 – 3,000 MHz	

area, it's likely that some stations will maintain broadcasting and that people who have higher quality receiving equipment will be able to receive the signals.

Government Radio Services

Government services are both broadcast (sent to many listeners) and point-to-point (two-way radio). In either case, the ability to eavesdrop can be valuable. Typical of these are the weather radio service, air traffic control and marine radio service. Most amateur radio supply houses sell a fairly inexpensive circuit board that, when installed in a PC and coupled to an antenna, will allow a person to receive satellite weather pictures.

Scanners

Scanners are listen-only devices that search VHF and UHF frequencies. You can program the frequencies you want monitored. This is a good way to listen to emergency services. Even if you have a multiple channel VHF or UHF transceiver, it is good to have a scanner so you can monitor other channels while you are transmitting on a given channel.

International Short Wave Broadcasts

Short wave radios allow you to keep in touch with what is going on in other parts of the planet. Short wave radio broadcasts between 3 and 30 MHz can provide long-distance reception. This frequency of radio waves bounces off certain portions of the ionosphere. Short wave signals are clearer at night.

Many English language short wave DX radio stations are based outside the U.S., mostly from Europe. The BBC in the United Kingdom, the Swiss International Radio and the U.S. Armed Forces Radio network are among the most well-known. Good reception requires more sophisticated radio and antenna equipment, but information from foreign broadcasts may be very valuable during a national emergency.

The better grades of short wave receivers have what is called BFO. BFO is an option that enables the radio to receive single side band transmissions, tuning in ham operators from around the world. In the event of a national or international crisis, amateurs (hams) are the best source of direct and unprocessed news. Hams are real people who will generally tell you what is actually going on without the mass media's editorial filtering.

The Sangean ATS 909 gets good short wave reception and has the BFO option. It costs around $300. This radio will operate on batteries and for $60 more comes with a solar charging panel for daytime use.

The BayGen plus radio offers high performance and light when utility power is out. The radio will run for 40 hours when the internal battery pack is fully charged. The batteries are charged by winding, solar, or with the optional AC adapter.

The BayGen FreeplayPlus is a hand-powered, wind-up radio that receives short wave bands along with standard AM /FM reception. It has a built-in solar charging panel that will power the radio during the day and charge batteries at the same time; plus it includes a built-in flashlight! It costs about $100 from Yellowstone Trading.

Transmitting

There are many options for radios that both transmit and receive. Determining who you want to communicate with can narrow the choice. At a minimum, a family should be able to connect with other families in their area. This could mean an inexpensive CB radio, commercial VHF or UHF, amateur 2-meter ham, FRS, GMRS and even marine band. For transmitting longer distances, the only option will be amateur ham equipment that operates in the lower frequency range. This requires training to be a licensed operator with the right equipment. So for most families, transmitting options are limited to CB and commercial VHF and UHF.

FRS Band

A relatively new option is the Family Radio Service (FRS) Band that was set aside by the FCC and defined as "a low power ($^1/_2$ watt), short range UHF service established to meet the communication needs of families and groups." No license is required. The 14 FRS channels are located between standard GMRS (General Mobile Radio Service) channels. This appears to be ideal for people separated by short distances, from 5 to 12 miles, depending on the terrain. They cost from $80 to $140 and can be purchased from numerous sources including Radio Shack and Cabelas.

GMRS

Family radios fill a great need, but they have their limits when it comes to distance. On the other hand, General Mobile Radio Service (GMRS) handheld radios provide increased wattage (4 watts) facilitating longer-range communications. Some, like the ClearConnect, can use GMRS repeaters, providing a potential 25-mile range. They have the 462.675 MHz emergency and motorist assistance channel.

Handheld radios can help maintain contact with family members. Modern models broadcast over greater distances, up to 12 miles under optimal conditions.

The ClearConnect has another unique feature, a BNC antenna connector that can attach to an exterior-mounted antenna via a coaxial cable to be mounted on a car roof or an underground shelter. All of the FRS radios have fixed antennas. BNC connector facilitates two-way communications from inside the shelter with a surface-mounted exterior antenna. The ClearConnect GMRS has 23 channels; channels 1–7 are the same as Family Radio channels 1–7. This allows communication with FRS radios (at higher wattage). Like the FRS radios, all of the GMRS channels are preprogrammed. Midland makes a line of GMRS radios that includes a lesser priced, non-repeater model.

GMRS radios require an FCC use license, which can be applied for over the Internet.

The large number of CB radio operators make owning a CB an effective local news resource.

Citizens Band

Citizens Band (CB) radios are inexpensive and common nationwide. CB radio service is in the 27 Megahertz band. They operate at 5 watts, limiting them to local communication. A more expensive variety of CB radio is the CB Side Band radio which operates at 12 watts allowing it to transmit farther than the conventional 5 watt CB.

All CB radios use the same channel frequencies and therefore can talk to each other. This is not the case with commercial VHF and UHF radios that have specifically assigned and licensed frequencies. So CB communication is less private.

Commercial VHF and UHF

State, city and county emergency services use designated frequencies within the VHF and UHF frequency ranges. The VHF uses a low band of 32 to 49 MHz. Emergency services used to be in this area, but most have moved up to high band VHF.

There is a lot of inexpensive, used low band equipment floating around. This low band equipment will potentially transmit farther because of the lower frequency but it is just about all crystal equipment. The expense of re-crystalling the radio is three-quarters of the cost of a good synthesized radio. The only way to make effective use of this old equipment is to be able to get a license for the frequency that the radio is already crystalled for.

Commercial VHF and UHF frequencies are licensed. You can apply for your own licensed frequency that can then be programmed into radios in the neighborhood.

Commercial VHF and UHF radio equipment is available but reasonably expensive. This equipment is characterized by its simplicity of operation. These radios are generally not field-programmable like similar amateur radios. Field-programmable means you can program frequencies into the radio channels with the radio itself. Commercial equipment usually must be taken to a service shop to have new frequencies installed. Recently a number of companies have come out with field-programmable handheld VHF radios. These include King, Relm, Motorola and Icom.

Field-programmable radios are a desirable option. During an emergency situation, a person can't just run down to the local radio shop to have a new frequency programmed into the radio.

Relm makes a 16 channel 25-watt VHF field programmable mobile unit. Other than size, the main difference between a handheld and a mobile radio is power. Hand-held radios do not have much transmission power (no more than 5 watts) and thus they can't transmit messages any great distance. Mobile VHF and UHF radios usually start at 25 watts and go up to 40 and 100 watts. Falcon Direct sells a unit that boosts a 25-watt radio to 100 watts for about $300.

Commercial radios are usually fairly expensive. One exception is the ProConnect 99, at about $169 (and it is not made in China)! This two-way radio is available in either VHF or a UHF model. The ProConnect is not field programmable, but the programming module is relatively inexpensive.

Another alternative to expensive commercial radios are field programmable amateur radios. Dual band radios can transmit and receive on both VHF and UHF. The frequency bands reserved for use by licensed amateur radio operators are discussed later in this chapter.

Marine Band Radios

Marine Band radios are another option. Federal Communication Commission (FCC) regulations prohibit their use on land, but during a disaster this may not be a concern. However, don't plan on using them during non-disaster times. Marine band radios are very inexpensive.

Amateur Radio Service

Amateur radio is the oldest, most flexible and therefore most useful radio service. Amateur radio frequency bands are spotted throughout the radio spectrum. An amateur license requires passing an FCC exam. Licensed amateurs can communicate locally, nationally and internationally. This service offers the possibility for a number of communicating modes, such as voice, telegraphy, teletype and packet.

In the 30 Mhz or less lower frequency range, amateur radio makes use of single side band transmission to transmit farther with less wattage.

Amateur radio in combination with a local VHF, UHF and CB capability provides connection with the world and the local area. One amateur can keep a whole community informed.

Amateur radio operators (hams) have a wealth of knowledge. In almost every reasonably sized city in the United States there is an Amateur Radio Club. These clubs put on courses for people who want to get their amateur licensing. Local hams are a good source of information and advice. They can be a great help in locating used equipment.

The American Radio Relay League offers, for $30, a great communications resource: the *ARRL Handbook*.

FCC

The FCC strictly enforces its rules. For example, anyone caught operating without a license gets an $8,000 fine. Anyone using an unauthorized frequency gets a $5,000 fine. Even hindering an inspection by a FCC agent is a $7,500 fine. The FCC does not need a search warrant. Above and beyond fines, the FCC can confiscate any equipment involved in the violation. The local hams monitor radio traffic on most of the frequencies and commonly turn in unauthorized users to the FCC.

However, there are some exceptions to required licensing for transmitting on some amateur frequencies in an emergency.

Contact your local County Disaster and Emergency Services Office (DES) and ask them if you can get permission to communicate with them in the event of an emergency on their designated state frequency. Also ask them if you can get permission to transmit on your state's "common" mutual aid channel. Almost all law enforcement, fire, emergency medical services and DES radios scan this frequency.

Antennas

An antenna system is part of every radio set-up. A separate antenna is required for every radio.

They can take several forms; a long horizontal wire attached to two vertical supports, a vertical rod or mast fixed to a ground support or a tower with a directionally controlled beam array.

Directional beam antennas allow a radio operator to concentrate receiving capability in a given direction and thus receive a distant, weak transmission that would otherwise be drowned out by competing signals from other directions. This antenna requires a rotating device and position indicator.

A feedline connects the antenna to the radio equipment. Long feedline runs produce signal loss. High gain cable reduces the effect of this signal loss.

Antennas are tuned for limited frequency ranges. A broad-band antenna will do a mediocre job of receiving and transmitting on a number of different frequencies where a specifically tuned antenna will give excellent transmission and reception on a limited spectrum of frequency.

There is no one perfect radio or all-purpose antenna. With this information you can choose what best fits your needs, time and budget.

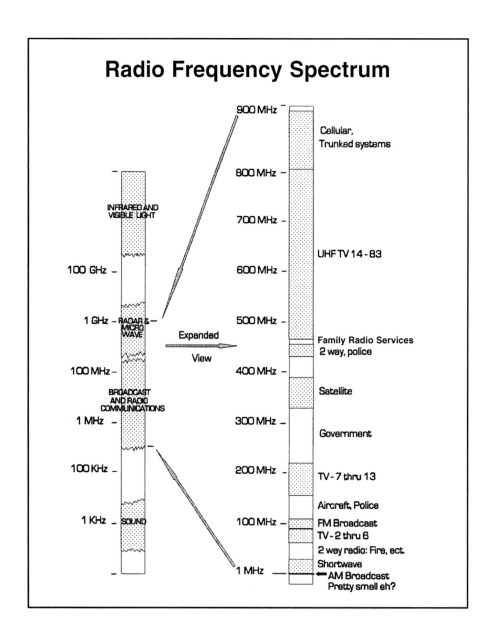

CHAPTER 10
Evacuation Scenario

The Longwells

"It looks like another scorcher," Patrick told himself, as he got ready to take his family on a 4th of July picnic. This was the third year in a row that they had had drought conditions in Sacramento. As a result, there was not enough water to keep the lawns green and the area outside the city limits was incredibly dry.

As he loaded lawn chairs into the back of the minivan, he heard fire engine sirens in the distance. "Oh no!" he thought. "This place is such a tinderbox, any fire could be a real problem." To make matters worse, there was a hot dry wind blowing.

Patrick's wife Melanie was inside gathering food and trying to organize the children. The two younger girls were watching cartoons on the local TV station. Suddenly the program was interrupted by a news broadcast talking about a fire that had started from fireworks in an area just outside of town. The wind had carried it into a grove of trees and from there it was racing out of control toward the edge of town. Melanie watched with concern as she realized it was headed for their neighborhood.

The MacDonalds

Just down the road a quarter of a mile, John MacDonald was loading his golf clubs into the car for a morning game of golf with his buddies. They wanted to get out before it got too hot. He also heard the sirens but hadn't paid them much attention. He really wanted to get out to the green. His wife was visiting her ailing parents in the Bay area. Their two sons had spent the night at a friend's house and weren't expected home until later on in the afternoon. He finally had a day out with the guys.

As he drove, John turned on the radio. He half listened as the disc jockey mentioned a large fire burning in the fields outside of town. He wasn't worried. He knew the fire department was on it. Isn't that what he paid taxes for?

The Longwells

Melanie called to Patrick and he came in to watch the news. Patrick was alarmed. The situation portrayed on TV matched his greatest fears. The fire was growing fast. The wind was directing it toward a section of houses on the edge of the city right where they lived. The newscast mentioned the possibility of evacuation. By this time, the whole family was gathered around the TV. They watched in stunned silence for a few moments, trying to take in the whole situation.

"Okay," said Melanie finally, breaking the silence. "Let's get ready to evacuate in case it comes to that." The three children stared at their mother, trying to determine if she was really serious. By the look on her face, they all decided she was.

Patrick hurried to the car, pulled out the lawn chairs and the bag of charcoal and then hurried back into the house. He opened the hall closet and took out two backpacks. Although they were heavy, he carried one in each hand and loaded them into the back of the car. The three children came out each carrying an overstuffed daypack to add to what was already in the car.

Melanie grabbed some empty cardboard boxes from the garage. "We have time for everyone to load up one box with what they would like to take with them," Melanie instructed the children. The three of them went off to their rooms, numbed from the fear they felt rising up inside them, yet comforted that their parents seemed to know what to do.

The MacDonalds

John MacDonald arrived at the golf course. "Hey, we didn't expect to see you here," commented one of his friends. "Didn't you hear about the fire? It's totally out of control. They might need to evacuate your neighborhood. "

John was stunned. "Why did they let that happen," he managed to mutter. "I guess I better head back and see what's up."

When John neared home he couldn't believe the smoke. It was really thick. He could now see the flames, leaping high in an area that must be no more than two miles away. As he turned onto his street he could see neighbors carrying armloads of stuff to their cars.

John pulled into his driveway. Their friend's mom had just dropped off his two sons, ages six and eight.

"Dad, what are we going to do," they asked in voices filled with fear.

John stood just inside the front door and glanced around the house. He felt totally unprepared for this. He really wished his wife Susan was here. He had no idea where to start. His sons raced uncontrollably around the house, hyped up by both excitement and fear.

The Longwells

"We can take Zip, Tigger and Mischief, can't we?" the children pleaded. "Of course," responded Patrick. "Put the cats in their carrier. Bring along some food for them." One of the cats could not be found right away and the children were becoming hysterical. However, by the time the car was packed, Tigger finally responded to the children's insistent calling and ambled into the yard.

The TV was no longer working. The electricity had gone out.

Patrick and Melanie had already decided they were going to evacuate. They felt pretty good about what they had with them even though they were sick about the possibility of losing their house, their furniture and everything else.

Six months before they had made the decision to prepare for a possible evacuation. "It's happened to other people. It could happen to us." They had been surprised at how simple it was to put together a 72-hour backpack for everyone. Patrick and Melanie's packs included some lightweight camping pads, tent, first aid kit, and a windup radio, along with the essentials in everyone else's packs: water, dehydrated meals in pouches, flashlights, extra clothes and a light sleeping bag.

They started driving, Melanie noticed with relief that they had $3/4$ of a tank of gas. They switched on the car radio. They were in a residential area and there still wasn't much traffic.

The authorities were telling everyone to evacuate as soon as possible. The area to be evacuated had grown now to a whole section running along the length of the city's west side. It was obvious that they were getting out ahead of the crowd. They had to drive into the city to move away from the fire. The roads were reasonably clear. They drove along in silence, feeling tense but grateful. They knew they were safe and could take care of themselves.

The MacDonalds

John opened the refrigerator and stared blankly at its contents. There didn't seem to be much that was ready to eat. He pulled out some sandwich fixings and put them into a bag. He decided to leave the beer. He grabbed some snack food from the cupboard. As he turned to leave the kitchen, he thought about something to drink. He turned on the faucet. There was still water coming out. Great! After rummaging around for a minute, he located some discarded pop bottles and filled these up with water. "Okay, what's next?" he thought to himself.

Just then he heard a voice from a loudspeaker coming from the street. "Please evacuate your home now!" said the patrolman from his car as he drove slowly down the street.

John was surprised. "Surely they would give him more time than this," he told himself. He hurried into the boys' room and threw some clothes into a bag. "Take this to the car," he told his oldest son.

"I'm not leaving without Skipper," the boy replied frantically but firmly. "If you can find him, we'll take him," John answered, his anxiety level rising by the moment. John wished he could call his wife but the phones weren't working.

The patrol car was making a final sweep down his street as John dragged his boys to the car. Skipper, the family cat, had not shown up. As they started down the street John thought of all the other family treasures he had not had time to grab.

These thoughts were quickly replaced by the awareness that he was almost out of gas. As he neared the gas station he could see that every pump had a line of cars. John had no choice but to turn in and join the line. As he sat there waiting, he wondered how things had managed to get so out of control in so short a time.

CHAPTER 11

If You Need to Leave Your Home

Evacuation is no longer a highly unlikely scenario. Some people living in coastal cities have had direct experience with this situation. Even those of us who live in rural areas like Montana can imagine reasons why we might have to evacuate someday; for instance, forest fires or volcanic activity in Yellowstone.

With minimal prior planning, evacuation can be a smooth and successful procedure. It is certainly possible to live for a time away from home. People do it all the time when they go camping. Consider what is needed to support life if you have to leave home, camping without access to supermarkets or restaurants. The first chapters of this book cover the basics: pure water, food, light, warmth, if the climate and season dictates, and a way to receive news or other information regarding the disaster. Personal items, a first aid kit, knife, tube tent, sleeping bag can be added to the list to increase your comfort.

In the aftermath of Hurricane Katrina in the summer of 2005, when a second hurricane was threatening the same area, the mayor of New Orleans asked, "How hard is it to secure a 72-hour survival pack?" The emergency response to this unfortunate disaster taught us all that the government is not capable of taking care of us as well as we can take care of ourselves.

With a little planning and a few items in a backpack, your evacuation would be made immeasurably smoother and more comfortable. The stress of impending disaster does not lend itself to clear thinking. It is not the best time to be running around the house making decisions about what to take and what to leave behind. It is not the best time to be searching for that "working flashlight" or Tommy's left mitten or Susie's sunhat, or your bottle of Tylenol. Planning ahead prevents all this added stress.

72-hour Survival Kit

There are two options for securing a 72-hour survival kit. First, put together your own. This is the least expensive option but does require more effort. This chapter includes a list of what to put in a survival pack. The second option is to purchase one already made. This requires a bit more money but much less effort. There is no official standard for the contents of a 72-hour survival kit, so you need to do some research into what is available and put some thought into what you think you really need.

What is a 72-hour survival kit? The kit provides what you need to survive for three days. This kit is specifically valuable if you need to evacuate your home for any reason (flooding, earthquake, fire, hurricane, or terrorist attack). Store it in a convenient location so that you can grab it easily once you've made the decision to

A 72-hour survival pack could be your most valuable preparedness item.

evacuate. Although a 72-hour survival kit is perfect for evacuation, it would be a lifesaver in any emergency where you were at home but had no power. It covers the basic needs of water, food, light and communication.

When we at Yellowstone Trading first decided to put together a 72-hour survival kit, we researched what other kits were available, their contents and price. We found 72-hour survival kits that cost $29.99 and included barely anything, to kits that cost $600 and included everything but the kitchen sink and weighed accordingly. So we thought about what we would want to have with us if we needed to evacuate and put together a kit with these items.

Water

The first area is water. We suggest you store at least three 16 oz. water bottles right in your 72-hour survival pack. This size bottle is readily available. Use old juice or soft drink bottles if you like. Every six months fill them with fresh water. Pick two easy-to-remember days, like the 4th of July and New Year's.

Keep three pint water bottles full in your 72 hour survival pack.

Our 72-hour survival kit includes a bottle of Potable Aqua water purification tablets. We included the water purification tablets in the likely scenario that you would be near a water source, such as a stream, creek, river, lake, or spring. In an emergency, you can fill up your 16 oz. water bottle from the surface water, add one water purification tablet, and let the water sit for 30 minutes. These tablets will wipe out bacteria and other microorganisms, such as viruses and protozoa found in unsafe water, like Giardia. These Potable Aqua tablets are used by the U.S. military and are the favored method for water purification by outdoor enthusiasts who do not carry a water filter.

If you are using your kit to survive an emergency at home, the Potable Aqua tablets can be used to purify water from a hot water heater, water from pipes, and water from the tank of toilets (not the toilet bowl). Bad water kills more civilians in emergencies than the direct effects of the disaster itself.

If your budget will allow, a portable water filter is great idea. It provides nearly unlimited good drinking water as long as you are near a water source.

Food

Nutrition is especially important during an emergency. Under physical or emotional stress, good-tasting food is critical. Our kit features lightweight, nutritious dehydrated food, three meals for each of three days, plus three energy bars. The

AlpineAire pouches require no cooking; just add water (hot or cold) and eat.

additional 16 oz. of water per day needed to re-hydrate the food can either be carried or purified on the go. If you have children, having enough food is doubly important for them to function normally on an emotional and physical level.

Light

Efficient, lightweight, bright LED flashlights are economical and practical.

Light can be a life-saving tool. An emergency flashlight should be lightweight, bright and efficient. A wind-up or shake-up flashlight will never run out of light yet these are a bit heavy. A lightweight, aluminum, LED flashlight is so long-lasting that with one extra set of batteries it will run for 40 hours. LED bulbs do not break. The addition of a 36-hour candle provides light, heat (no cold hands) and cooking. Being able to heat up water to re-hydrate your meals (most will re-hydrate with cold water too) will provide a large degree of comfort, especially if the temperature is cold.

Communication

When normal communication systems are cut off, the only reliable source of knowledge is a radio. The radio provides access to emergency broadcasts put out by police, government agencies and emer-

The Kaito lightweight, wind-up, solar powered AM/FM/SW radio provides a reliable source for news and emergency information.

gency personnel. Emergency broadcasts provide information to make good decisions, perhaps to evacuate, or the availability of food, shelter, and medical care.

Choose a radio that is either solar or wind-up for maximum reliability. Some radios offer a choice of four energy sources: AC adapter, battery pack, solar and hand crank.

This 72-hour survival pack is available from Yellowstone Trading. The individual components are available separately.

When You Receive the Word to Evacuate

The evacuation experience can vary widely, depending on preparation and the circumstances. You might find yourself calmly putting your 72-hour survival kit into your car and driving casually down the road to safety. Advance preparation could mean you are in front of the crowd when it comes time to leave.

Keep your survival pack in an accessible location, like the hall closet. You may also want to keep a pack in the trunk of your car.

Keeping the gas tank in your car at least half full at all times will ensure that you have the best chance of making it out of the danger area without getting stuck at a gas station behind a long line of cars. Fill up when you are half empty, especially during times of potential threat. Many disasters occur without warning. It would be easy to store 10 to 20 gallons of gasoline in your garage. Adding a fuel preservative such as PRI will ensure that the gasoline stays fresh.

On the other hand, you might find yourself needing to evacuate on foot, taking only what you can carry on your back. Despite your best preparations, an earthquake, fire, or other sudden emergency can demand that an area be evacuated quickly and the roads may be damaged or closed. If you have carefully planned ahead of time and packed as lightly as possible, you will find that you can accomplish this form of evacuation as well. If you have practiced carrying your survival pack prior to an emergency, you will be familiar with your pack. Having confidence makes for clear decisions and a calm family. Children benefit from the experience of carrying their packs and will generally enjoy practice times.

The best 72-hour survival pack doesn't work as well if items are missing; never borrow items from the pack during non-emergency times. This takes some self-control. Have a clear understanding with all family members that everything in the pack is off-limits except during emergencies. You may need duplicate flashlights, warm hats, and sleeping bags.

No matter what the emergency, having a pack ready will not only increase your safety and comfort, it will give you the peace of mind that comes from knowing you have done your best to prepare.

Checklist for a 72-Hour Survival Kit

Water – (16 oz. a day for each person) and either water purification tablets or a portable water filter

Food – (9 meals per person) Backpacking meals that require no cooking are best. Consider weight. More water will be needed to re-hydrate this food.

Light – Flashlight with extra bulb and batteries (if flashlight requires batteries). Most reliable are either an LED windup flashlight or a shakeup flashlight.

Radio – Radio with extra batteries (if required). Windup and solar powered radios are the most dependable.

Matches/Lighter

Silverware

Small Knife

First Aid Kit w/Basic First Aid Booklet

Cash

Copies of important papers:

- Birth Certificates

- Ownership papers for your home and vehicles

- Insurance papers: auto, home, and life

- Phone numbers for family members and friends

Toiletries

Wet wipes/Toilet paper

Extra clothes (appropriate for your area and the season); hat, gloves

Poncho/Large garbage bags (for multiple uses including rain gear, garbage collection, or ground cloth)

Day Pack or Backpack

Consider:

Tent or tarp and nylon rope

Sleeping bag/Camping pad

Signal Mirror

Sierra Cup (for heating water)

36-hour candle with folding stove

Hand warmers

Folding shovel/Trowel

Dust mask/Latex gloves

Protein bars

E-mergen-C energy drink packets

Small sewing kit

Note: A complete checklist for all your preparations can be found on page 5.

CHAPTER 12

Power Generation

Electrical power is essential to our standard of living and use of technology. Unfortunately, the national electrical distribution grid is vulnerable to the effects of rolling blackouts, war and major natural disaster. We take for granted the power that this system provides.

If the electricity stops, our lives will radically change. Most people won't have running water. The average person won't be able to get a drink of water or flush the toilet. Most people won't have heat. The exception is the person who has a wood stove. (Pellet stoves, on the other hand, require electricity.) Natural gas and propane furnaces require electricity to operate their burner assemblies and blowers. Most communication systems require power. Practically all of our medical services are supported by electric power.

Using electricity from the power grid is a no-hassle, no-maintenance endeavor. If the lights go out you telephone the power company and someone else comes out to fix the problem. Power company customers use

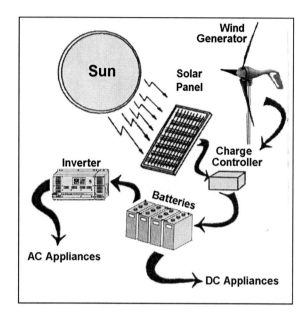

whatever power they want whenever they want it.

Changing to an alternative power generating system forces lifestyle changes. Independent systems require user involvement. If you do not maintain and repair, when necessary, your independent power generating system, eventually you'll no longer have power. Independent power systems necessitate that daily routines have to conform to the capacity of the power generating system. This means conservation and scheduling.

Alternative energy sources, such as solar, hydropower and wind, have advantages. They don't depend on a fuel tank that may eventually run dry. The down side to renewable energy sources is that they are expensive and they don't generally produce as much continuous electrical power as a fuel-run generator.

Some people entertain the idea of using a battery system that is charged from the electrical grid as a power failure backup. This is all right on a short-term basis, but such a system can only supply minimal power, and it ultimately needs to be recharged.

A basic understanding of electrical systems and terms is required to choose an alternative system that meets individual needs. Independent power generation is not all that complex; it's just that with the grid's relative reliability and convenience, most people these days haven't had to focus their attention on generating power. The exceptions are those who have remote cabins, RVs, marine applications or alternative energy inclinations. A basic understanding of electrical systems is important so that people can maintain and troubleshoot their generator, battery bank and inverter systems during an emergency.

Definitions of electrical terms are at the end of this chapter.

Independent Power Systems

Solar Power

The photovoltaic effect involves light particles striking the solar panel material to produce a flow of electrons. Sunlight on solar panel material causes electrons to excite. The solar voltaic cell collects a percentage of these

Solar panels provide a reliable, renewable energy source.

excited electrons and directs them to flow in a path. The flow of electrons in a path is defined as electricity.

Photovoltaic modules, or solar panels as they are called, collect and convert sunlight into DC electrical power. Wires carry this DC electricity to a battery bank where it is stored. On the way to the batteries, the electrical current passes through a controller (regulator) which shuts off the flow when the batteries are fully charged. Solar panels need to produce at least 15 or 16 volts to charge a 12-volt battery.

Wind-Powered Generators

Just as sun is required for solar power, in order to use wind you have to live in an area with lots of wind. And like solar, if you want lots of power you are going to need lots of wind turbines, which means lots of money. Wind-powered generator systems can be used to charge battery banks. Wind generated electrical power can be used directly without the use of batteries for pumping water. Wind-powered generators can be the sole source of power in a system, or they can be part of a hybrid system, supplementing other power sources.

Consistent wind is critical. In many areas wind is seasonal. As a rule of thumb, any area with an average wind speed of 12 mph has good wind power generating potential.

Windmills are another option for energy independence.

To find out how many watts of power the wind

can generate, cube the wind speed. A 20 mile per hour wind can generate 8000 watts (20 x 20 x 20 = 8000). If the wind speed doubles (40 miles per hour), the electrical power generated by the wind increases eight times (40 x 40 x 40 = 64,000). A site with extreme wind speed fluctuations has at least twice the electrical power generating potential of a site that has a consistent, but moderate, wind speed. Occasional high wind speeds have a lot of electrical power. These occasional high wind speeds must be frequent enough to keep the

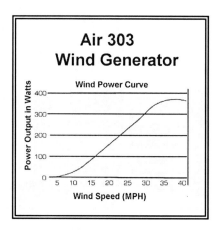

batteries charged. Or there are wind-powered generators that are made especially to operate effectively in areas with slower constant wind speeds.

Because of line loss, solar panels and wind generators cannot be placed at an excessive distance from the battery bank.

Hydroelectric Generators

Hydroelectric power requires water and lots of it. Second you need a major change in elevation. It is by tapping into a water flow at a higher elevation and piping it down to a lower elevation through a series of pipe reductions that you create the pressure necessary to power a water turbine. The third requirement is a state permit to tap into the water, which is getting harder to obtain because of environmental legislation.

AC hydroelectric generator systems are typically large and expensive. Another problem is the AC power they produce cannot be stored unless it is converted to DC and put in a battery bank. Consequently, AC units must be capable of generating enough power to meet the demands of the peak loads. Sizing a unit for peak loads requires up to 40 times more water than a similarly useful DC system that accumulates energy into a battery bank over a 24-hour period.

The smaller scale DC units cost about $1000. Harris manufactures an

Gallons of Water per Minute	Harris Model # of Heads	Feet of Head (elevation difference between water source and turbine)						
		25'	50'	75'	100'	200'	300'	600'
3	One					40	70	150
6				10	20	100	150	300
10			15	45	75	180	275	550
15			50	85	120	260	400	800
20	Two	25	75	125	190	375	550	1100
30		50	125	200	285	580	800	1500
50	Four	115	230	350	500	800	1200	
100		200	425	425	850	1500		
200			515	850	1300			

Hydroelectric DC Generator Potential in Watts

efficient, durable battery-charging Pelton turbine in both 12- and 24-volt configurations that are well suited for use on smaller creeks and springs. The 12- or 24-volt power can be used directly from the batteries to operate DC low voltage lights and appliances or can be routed through an inverter to provide 110-volt AC. Both configurations are compatible for use with other DC charging systems such as solar and gas generators.

Steam Generators

Steam, as with other forms of alternate energy, has its own application and advantages. If you have access to an abundance of combustible raw materials such as wood, paper, coal, oil, corncobs, straw, or trash, steam may be a workable option. Heat is a by-product from steam power generation. Exhaust heat from a steam plant can be used for co-generation, such as heating domestic water or heating a building. Wind, photovoltaic and hydropower systems do not produce waste heat.

Mike Brown Steam Engine

Steam power requires more work than wind or solar. Steam generation requires a continual supply of large quantities of wood, coal or other burnable waste products. Much labor is involved in cutting, hauling and feeding the boiler with wood or other burnable substance. In addition, steam engines are not cheap.

The challenge of hydro and steam is to generate enough power to meet the demands of the peak loads. Sizing a hydro unit for peak loads requires a lot of water, and sizing a 10 kW steam generator for peak loads will require a cord of wood for three days of running time. Pretty soon there could be no more trees in your neighborhood. But a 500-watt DC steam generator only consumes 20 pounds of wood an hour.

The nice aspect of the DC option is that you have control over the power output. When you want power you build a fire and you can use a smaller unit to charge up the battery bank over a longer period of time.

A 500-watt DC steam generator sells for $2,000 to $3,000. A 10,000-watt AC unit costs about $15,000. The larger units are cheaper per watt. You have the option of using a smaller, less expensive unit and running it for a longer time.

A 1 horsepower steam engine is capable of putting out enough power to drive a 500-watt generator, depending on the pressure from your boiler. The advantage to the steam generator is that it has the potential to keep going when other generators run out of gasoline and diesel fuel. With the steam generator, you are not at the mercy of the elements. There are only so many hours of sun a day and most of us can't control the wind.

AC Generators

Liquid fuel-powered generators provide reliable power generation, as long as the fuel lasts. This generator is not affected by an absence of wind or sunshine. Three fuel options are propane, diesel and gasoline. Each fuel option has its pros and cons.

The prices of gasoline, natural gas, propane and diesel will probably continue to rise. Worse yet, these fuels may eventually become unavailable. The only solution to unavailability is storage and we will thoroughly discuss this issue later in this chapter. The distribution of natural gas is dependent on the electrical grid. If the grid goes down, so eventually will natural gas pressure. If the roads or distribution networks are challenged, fuel delivery of any sort will suffer.

Diesel

Diesel is the fuel of choice. It is not explosive and if stored below ground with the proper anti-fungal treatment will last 20 years. Diesel generators last longer than gas-powered generators, but cost considerably more.

Chinese-made diesel generators are relatively inexpensive, but they are fairly noisy and they don't have an industrial performance track record. Yanmar and Kubota make the world's most efficient and dependable small diesel engines. Most of the diesel generators 5.5 kW or under are portable 2-pole 3600 rpm units. Water-cooled 1800 rpm units are available in 5.5 kW and up. These 1800 rpm units are industrial and last longer due to their slower speed. Deutz is another excellent manufacturer. Deutz diesel generators are air-cooled generators made in West Germany. Deutz diesels start at 18 kW. China Diesel copied the Deutz design. Perkins is an excellent mid-range, water-cooled British-made diesel.

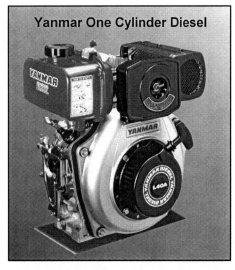

Yanmar One Cylinder Diesel

Generators provide reliable back-up power, at least for as long as the fuel supply lasts.

Gasoline

Gasoline-powered generators are inexpensive, but gasoline will separate and lose octane over time if a preservative is not added. Gasoline vapors are very explosive. Avoid gas generators if you can afford a diesel generator. A 5000-watt (5 kW) gasoline generator costs about $550 at a large discount or hardware store. The average performance life could be short—just 2000 hours.

Propane

Propane stores well, and will run many home appliances, including hot water heaters, cooking stoves, furnaces, refrigerators and clothes dryers. Many people in rural settings already have a propane tank and use it for heat, cooking or hot water.

Propane powered back-up generator packages are user-friendly, self-contained and uncomplicated to install. They are built specifically to provide back-up power in the event the local power supply fails. Propane generators cost less than their comparable diesel counterparts, but their expected life span is less. Gasoline engines can be converted to propane. A converted gasoline engine will not operate as efficiently as an engine that was built specifically for propane. Propane engines have a different compression ratio and many times different valve guides.

Safety is another issue. Propane conversion kits are getting harder to find because most manufacturers will only do propane adaptations at the factory due to liability issues. Search the Internet for current sources for propane conversion kits.

CAUTION: Propane is heavier than air and very explosive; hence it should not be used in underground confined areas. A propane explosion in an underground shelter would be disastrous. For use in an underground shelter, provide a drain to daylight under every LPG appliance and use LPG sensors.

Natural Gas

Natural gas seems to be a logical option for powering an emergency generator in an area that is serviced by a natural gas pipeline. However, the compressor stations on the natural gas pipeline require power from the electrical grid. Regional power shortages, war, or natural disaster could disrupt the national electrical grid that would cause an eventual loss of natural gas pressure. Also in the event of nuclear war, an electromagnetic pulse could fry the microprocessors that control the natural gas compressor stations.

Fuel Efficiency

A diesel-powered generator consumes one gallon of diesel fuel to produce 10,000 watts of power for one hour. A gasoline generator uses twice the gas, a propane generator needs three times as much propane, and a natural gas-powered generator requires four gallons, all for the same power.

Long-term Fuel Storage

Underground Tanks

One drawback to gasoline and diesel is that they are environmentally hazardous liquids. Underground tank storage is expensive and new EPA regulations strictly control the installation of underground fuel storage tanks. In most cases, the installation of an underground tank will have to be done by a state licensed tank installer. This makes the underground tank option too expensive for most non-commercial users.

Underground gasoline and diesel tanks must also have vapor monitoring wells. Vapor monitoring has to be done monthly using an expensive vapor-monitoring device; there are businesses that provide this service.

The best way to lessen the chances of an accidental fuel loss is to stringently adhere to the standards that experts in the industry formulated. The cost of a fuel spill cleanup is beyond most people's means. Taking shortcuts or having non-certified people do tank and piping installations increases the chances of a system failure.

Alternative Fuel Storage

There are inexpensive and durable alternatives to underground fuel storage tanks. On a small scale, there are five-gallon military surplus "Jerry-cans." But you'll need a lot of them if your fuel supply needs are great. Consider portable plastic fuel tanks on wheels (typically 20-gallon size) available at marine supply. Another option is auxiliary tanks for large diesel trucks and pickups. Large surface storage tanks have capacities of 250 gallons plus. Check with commercial fuel suppliers to find sources that lease or sell these tanks. Bargain-priced tanks may be found through classified ads listing industrial equipment auctions.

Try to place your fuel in a cool, shaded area, like a shed. Heat from sunlight will speed the oxidative process, and temperature swings cause condensation to build, resulting in water accumulation in tank bottoms.

If you choose a larger aboveground tank, make sure it is equipped with a valve on the tank bottom so that you can periodically drain any water accumulation. Keep your tank topped off leaving about five percent of capacity free for headspace. This minimizes condensation, yet allows the fuel to expand and contract with temperature variances.

One of the best fuel storage options is a fuel tank inside of a tank, culvert or concrete crypt belowground. The fuel tank needs to have enough space around it so it can be inspected. The tank, culvert or concrete crypt should be water or fuel tight to contain any leak. Such a fuel storage system is not considered an underground buried fuel tank and should not come under regulations for underground fuel tanks.

Another option is to dig a hole and have a concrete water cistern installed with a manhole entry. These are manufactured by the companies that make septic tanks. These companies have trucks that can deliver and place the concrete tank in the hole. Then construct a pallet-like floor on the concrete floor of the water cistern. Put empty fuel-grade steel 55-gallon drums in the prepared water cistern, then fill the drums with fuel. The slightly elevated wooden floor will prevent the bottom of the steel drums from contacting the concrete floor and reduce the chance of rusting. The tank will contain the fuel in the event of a leak, and being underground keeps the fuel cool and out of sight.

Diesel fuel can be stored inside a structure. In the case of a structure like an underground fallout shelter, fuel could be stored in barrels and tanks as long as they can be inspected for leakage. The room should have a floor that could contain a spill without it leaking into the ground. This room should be isolated from the rest of the shelter with a fireproof/ vapor-proof door. Diesel fuel can be purchased for off-road use from the local bulk plant. If privacy is a concern, the bulk plant will fill any tank or barrel that you bring in the back of a truck.

Consult the local fire marshal regarding the inside storage of diesel fuel.

Fuel Degeneration

Fresh fuel can go bad in just a matter of weeks. However, there are measures you can take to ensure fuel longevity. Approximately 70 percent of all back-up generator failures are fuel-related due to the oxidative process. Oxidation causes fuel to develop gum, resin and varnish.

Gasoline usually contains constituents that are subject to oxidation. This results in the formation of gums and a reduction in octane. Diesel fuel is more stable than gasoline, but it does have its own share of storage problems, most notably algae build-up.

Diesel fuel tends to accumulate water that condenses out of the air and collects in the bottom of the tank. In addition, the interface between the layers of fuel and water provides all the nutrients that microorganisms need to grow and multiply. These microorganisms produce acids that corrode metal components and create waste products that block fuel lines, clog filters, and foul entire fuel systems with sludge. Diesel fuel stored undisturbed for long periods is especially vulnerable to this microbial infestation.

The new so-called "clean" fuels typically deteriorate much faster than fuels made 20 years ago. This includes the new EPA mandated reformulated gasoline, (RFG), that contains oxygenate additives, derivatives of methyl alcohol and ethyl alcohol, and the new EPA mandated low-sulfur diesel fuel. Another factor is the new efficient processing techniques used by fuel refiners. The new refinery techniques produce more gasoline per barrel of crude, but the fuels are often far less stable and sometimes are out of spec for stability by the time they reach your tank. The same stability issues hold true for the new generation of diesel fuels. They are lower in sulfur content, but less stable.

Whether diesel or gasoline, there is no way of knowing just how stable your fuel is unless you run expensive oxidation stability tests. One day you can get a fairly good fuel, and the next day it can be marginal or even way out of specification. Even if you go to the trouble and expense of testing your fuel, by the time the test results come back with a positive result, the fuel may have degenerated below specification.

Another factor is the quality of the crude oil feedstock going into the refinery changes with each shipment. Processing equipment must be precisely adjusted to the varied quality of the crude, but this does not always happen. Thus, the end result is poorly processed, less stable fuels. One oil company survey reports that more than half of all gasoline sold today is substandard.

Fuel Preservatives

PRI is the best choice in a fuel preservative.

Optimum storage environment solves 50 percent of the fuel degradation problem. But even with optimum physical storage conditions, fuel will still degrade without proper fuel treatment. There are a number of fuel preservatives that do a fair to poor job of preserving fuel over a long period of time.

However, one product, PRI, is very effective. PRI is an industrial-grade fuel preservative that stabilizes diesel fuel, kerosene and gasoline. PRI has been used for years in the industrial marine industry and is now available to retail consumers.

PRI makes PRI-D for diesel and PRI-G for gasoline. Tests have demonstrated that PRI can restore stale fuels to a refinery-fresh condition. In one case, some 15-year-old gas was taken from a car in a junkyard in New Hampshire. The sample was sent to Saybolt Laboratories in Boston for analysis. Predictably, the fuel was completely unusable when tested for oxidation stability. The gasoline was then treated with PRI-G and re-tested. The test result showed that PRI-G treatment restored the bad fuel to a refinery fresh specification.

PRI-D eliminates algae growth in diesel fuel tanks. It safely dissolves algae and other sludge and gums that have built up inside the fuel tank. PRI-D and PRI-G can be purchased from Yellowstone Trading.

Any liquid hydrocarbon fuel that has been stored for a long time should be filtered through a fine filter before use. This is especially true with diesel fuel, which needs both sediment and water removed from the fuel. Racor makes a full line of filter systems and water separator filters.

Generator Capacity

A generator's capacity to produce electrical energy is rated in terms of kilowatts (kW). A kilowatt equals 1,000 watts. Most generators are rated based on their capacity to meet a momentary surge and their continuous output capacity is generally less. Also, a generator's rating is based on performance at sea level. The real rating of a generator is 3.5 percent less for every additional 1,000 feet of altitude.

Selecting a Generator

In order to determine the proper generator size, make a list of the total wattage of all the tools, appliances and motors that will run at the same time. This total wattage should represent 70 percent of the generator's continuous wattage rating in order to achieve optimum fuel consumption efficiency and reduce premature engine wear. The temporary surge capacity represents what sort of power a generator can produce for a very short period of time. If run at its temporary rating for an extended period of time, the unit will probably burn up.

Check the nameplates on appliances and motors to determine wattage. If wattage is not shown, but amps and volts are given, use the formula Amps x Volts = Watts.

Example: 12.5 Amps x 120 Volts = 1500 Watts

Many loads have huge startup surge demands. Even though a total load may be 2500 watts, when the well pump starts up or the washing machine turns on a 5000-watt generator does not have enough capacity. Electric motors require three to four times the normal current to start.

Peak Loads and System Sizing

Map an electrical load schedule for a typical 24-hour period. This will help you to see what your peak loads are, when they occur and how, if possible, they can be rearranged or scheduled to balance the load during the time the generator is running. Two hours in the morning and two hours in the evening is a good option.

The second step is to fill out the "Electrical Demand Planning Worksheet" and the "Battery Sizing Worksheet" found in the Appendix. This includes all appliances, pumps, blowers, water heaters, cooling equipment, lights, radios, etc. Typical wattage requirements are also found in the Appendix.

When it comes to generators, bigger is not necessarily better. Diesel generators obtain maximum fuel efficiency when operating at about 70 percent of their rated capacity. When it comes to battery systems, bigger is better. Another battery consideration is the fact that batteries are only about 80 percent efficient. It takes 1.2 amp-hours of battery charging to

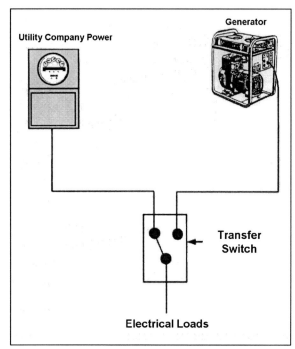

A transfer switch directs the source of a home's electricity between a home generator and the utility company.

produce 1 amp-hour of retrievable battery power.

Line Transfer Switch

A generator used for standby service requires a transfer switch between the utility power service and the generator. The transfer switch prevents the utility power from feeding into the generator and also prevents the generator from feeding out into the utility company's lines. This is intended to protect a serviceman who may be working on a damaged line. The line transfer switch should be installed by a qualified electrician.

There are four basic types of disconnect/transfer switches. The first and most basic system is an extension cord that runs from the generator to the appliance. This option does not interface with the house wiring or the main electrical panel.

The second option is a transfer switch placed in between the house's main electrical panel and the utility electrical supply line. This switch gives you the option of powering the entire house panel either off the generator or the grid.

The third option is a main panel with a built-in transfer switch. This panel has a mechanical connecting link between the main service breaker and the generator breaker. Turning one off automatically turns the other one on and vice versa.

The fourth option is a stand-alone transfer switch box with a load center incorporated into it. This unit is connected to the generator and has six or more breakers on it. Each breaker is connected to selected breakers in the main house electrical panel.

Utility power travels into the main house panel and then through the stand-alone transfer switch/load center before making an electrical run out to the circuit or appliance. In the event that the generator is turned on, all the user has to do is throw the appropriate breakers on the load center panel and the breaker is disconnected from utility power and powered with generator power.

AC or DC

Electrical power comes in two basic forms. The first is AC, alternating current, the standard power in most homes and businesses. With AC, the electrical current flow changes direction or alternates 50 to 60 times per second. The other form is DC, direct current. The lights and accessories in your car run on DC from the battery. Many of the appliances in recreational vehicles run on DC. With DC, the electrical current flows directly (in one direction). AC power is usually available in 110 and 220 volts. DC power systems usually operate in the 12-, 36- or 48-volt range.

One of the initial questions to be addressed is whether your home power system is going to operate off DC, AC, or both. One of the advantages of an AC system is that it will power conventional appliances that are relatively inexpensive. The other advantage to AC is that it is not subject to extreme line voltage loss.

DC power, between 12 and 36 volts, is a little safer than 110 to 220 volts AC, in regards to electrical shock. Also, DC power systems are generally made up of lower technology components making them less susceptible to the damaging effects of electro-magnetic pulse (EMP). Electrical wiring for DC systems is easier to install and less expensive than an AC system, as long as the system does not involve any long power line runs.

DC Power Choices: 12 vs. 24 or 48 Volts

The size of your electrical distribution configuration will determine the best voltage for your system. Small to medium systems lend themselves to 12 volts. The main problem with 12 volt is high line loss (see the wire loss tables in the Appendix).

Higher voltage ranges are especially good for medium to large systems. There is less line loss with 24 volts and even less with 48 volts. Larger capacity inverters are available, but it is not as easy to find 24- and 48-volt DC appliances. However, this disadvantage can be overcome by utilizing an inverter and regular AC appliances. The inverter utilizes conventional AC house wiring.

DC Voltage Line Loss

Long power line runs for DC systems are not efficient due to voltage line loss. The only solutions are to greatly increase the power cable diameter (at great expense) or increase the voltage.

A Wire Loss Table found at the end of the book in the Appendix shows the voltage loss experienced with various sized cables and at 120 AC and 12 and 24 volts DC. The tables shown are five percent tables, which means that at the listed amperage ratings and at the listed distances, five percent of the power would be lost to friction. A five percent voltage loss is normally acceptable in a low voltage system. If you desire a reduced voltage loss of two percent, divide the given distance by 2.5. For a 10 percent loss, multiply the distance by two. For a 48-volt system, double the 24-volt distances in order to obtain a five percent loss figure.

One consideration for a DC power system is that conventional AC household appliances won't work. Appliances have been developed to fill the needs of the RV (recreational vehicle) community and the marine industry. These DC appliances are much more expensive than AC appliances. On the plus side, DC appliances use less energy than AC appliances. In general, low voltage systems are not conducive to high-energy-use appliances and equipment. Blower fans and motors are two appliances that only work efficiently with AC. So energy conservation is an inherent part of low DC voltage electrical systems.

Generator Hybrid System

One practical solution to maintaining a stable power load system is a generator hybrid system. This involves coupling a generator to a battery charger, battery bank and an inverter. The battery charger operates whenever the generator is running and the inverter powers the AC loads whenever the generator is not running. There is a certain amount of efficiency loss

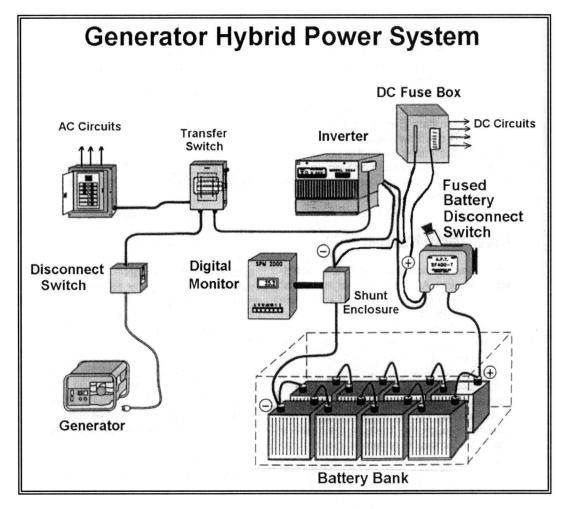

Generator Hybrid Power System

involved in changing or inverting battery-stored DC power to AC power with an inverter, but it is much more efficient than running a generator for long periods with only minimal loads.

Running a generator 24 hours a day is neither practical nor a good idea for most households. The most practical approach is to run a generator in the morning and evening and use a battery bank the rest of the time. When the generator is running the battery bank gets charged up. Run the AC appliances during the generator periods. Many AC appliances can be operated off the battery bank when the generator is not running. Some AC appliances are heavy power consumers and can't be powered by an

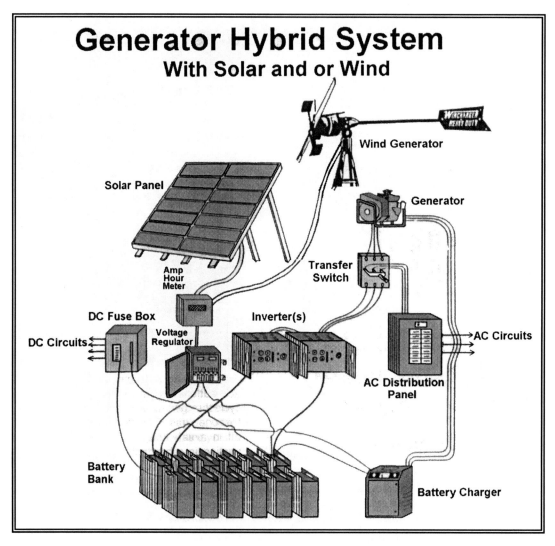

Generator Hybrid System
With Solar and or Wind

Wind Generator

Solar Panel

Generator

Amp Hour Meter

Transfer Switch

DC Fuse Box

Inverter(s)

Voltage Regulator

DC Circuits

AC Circuits

AC Distribution Panel

Battery Bank

Battery Charger

inverter. These heavy power consumers, such as well pumps and washing machines, will have to be scheduled for use during generator run times.

The chart at the end of this chapter describes the independent electrical power system components and their functions.

Inverters

Most household type appliances require "alternating current" or "AC" power. In some cases, appliances can use electricity pulled directly from the batteries. (This is where the term "direct current" comes from.) DC appliances include car headlights, flashlights, portable radios and DC-powered water pumps.

AC power can be produced by an inverter that transforms DC electricity into a higher voltage (usually 120 or 240) AC. Inverters produce alternating current (AC) from batteries that store direct current (DC).

Today's inverters are fairly bulletproof and in many cases they give cleaner electricity than from the grid. Newer, high capacity inverters have good surge demand capabilities, are 85 to 94 percent efficient and very reliable. (First generation inverters were inefficient and unreliable.) Most AC appliances and sensitive equipment like computers can be operated on power from true sine wave inverters.

In a limited sense, with an inverter, a person can have their cake and eat it too. Inverters bridge the gap between DC and AC systems. The inverter's AC output powers the circuit breaker box and the common outlets in a home.

Efficiency is the reason to operate selected loads at low voltage DC. Most new inverters only produce 120 volts AC, not the 120/240 volts AC that is typically drawn from the electrical utility grid. But when electrical heating appliances are replaced with gas appliances, there is very little need for 240 volts AC power.

Inverters have optimum efficiency operating in a range between 20 and 50 percent of their rated capacity. Inverters are not efficient when they are operating at a demand that is less than 10 percent of their rated capacity. Large, late generation inverters draw about 0.3 watts when they are in the idle mode. This same inverter will draw 10 to 15 watts when it has to start up and run a 2-watt load.

Inverter Sizing

Inverters, like fuel-powered generators, are rated in two ways: continuous wattage output rating and surge capacity rating. The necessary inverter continuous rating size can be determined by totaling the potential larger loads that could be operated at any given time. Typically, this could include the water pump, clothes washer, gas dryer and shop tools. It is important to make sure that the inverter has the surge capacity to start and run the appropriate combination of appliance loads at one time. For example, running the well pump and washing machine at the same time may not be a problem, but starting both at the same time could exceed the surge capacity of the system.

Power Waveform Problems

Inverters imitate the AC sine wave form. This is not a perfect imitation. There are two types of inverters on the market today, the modified sine wave inverter and the true sine wave inverter. Modified sine wave inverters cost less to buy. That translates to less cost per watt of power generated. These inverters do a fairly good job with the exception of computers and other delicate electronic appliances. True sine wave inverters produce electrical power that is virtually identical to the power supplied by the utility grid. True sine wave inverters cost more, but they will operate any appliance within their power range.

Some sophisticated electronic equipment with silicon controlled rectifiers do not like the power produced by modified sine wave inverters. Modified sine wave inverters can produce a buzz in radios and amplifiers. Inverters also broadcast radio noise, mainly on the AM band, which can interfere with reception if the radio is too close to the inverter.

Limitations

Most appliances will operate off inverter power as long as the inverter and the battery bank have sufficient capacity. But some equipment such as refrigerators, large motors, air conditioners, electric heaters and power tools are such exorbitant power consumers that they will in short order deplete the energy stored in the battery bank. Large inductive or split-phase type AC motors will draw up to six times their rated operating wattage when starting up. A typical $1/2$ horsepower motor can draw 6700 watts while starting up. In most cases, it would be best to have an AC generator that can be fired up when the need arises to directly power any of this type of equipment.

Inverter-Charger

Battery chargers are another converter consideration. A battery charger converts AC power into DC power. Trace makes a combination inverter/converter. Power running from the AC generator through the Trace unit into the batteries is converted to DC. DC power running from the batteries through the Trace unit to the electrical distribution system is inverted into AC.

An inverter is a piece of high-tech electronic equipment and is thus susceptible to being disabled or destroyed by electromagnetic pulse. To be protected from the threat of nuclear war, inverters should be shielded from EMP and have MOVs installed on all of the lines coming into and leaving the inverter. This is discussed in the book *No Such Thing as Doomsday.*

Ultimately, the question of providing continuous power generation versus operating off batteries is a question of system size and electrical demand. A low voltage DC power system's ability to deliver power on demand is limited by the size of the battery bank, the amount of electrical charge stored in the batteries, and the amount of power demanded by appliances.

When a generator is running, power is fairly abundant, but when the generator is off and the system runs off of battery power, scheduling and conservation come into play. Everyone with a low-voltage system needs to know how long they can operate various electrical appliances before they have to recharge the batteries, and how long they need to run the generator in order to fully charge the batteries. Charts and worksheets found in the Appendix will help with these calculations.

Batteries

Batteries are sensitive and expensive. Batteries are the weak link in an independent power system and require close attention and maintenance. Lead acid, deep-cycle batteries have life spans of five to eight years. We have seen thousands of dollars of battery investment go down the drain due to poor maintenance, self-discharge and freezing. Proper selection, installation, maintenance and charging of your battery bank will produce long life and trouble-free service.

When sizing your battery bank remember that bigger is better. A larger battery bank will last longer than a smaller one with similar loads because the demand is less on each individual battery, and you will have the ability to expand your system to handle unforeseen loads.

When shopping for batteries, the important factors to compare are how many amps will the battery deliver over a long slow discharge and how many times the battery can be cycled before it wears out. The battery's amp-hour rating and its cycle life are the primary factors which should be evaluated in choosing batteries for your power system.

Battery manufacturers rate their batteries at a particular hour rating. A 20-hour rating is the minimum standard for a battery to be used as part of an independent power system. A battery's energy storage capacity is rated in amp-hours. One amp of power supplied for one hour equals one amp-hour.

The capacity size of the battery bank depends on the demand of the electrical appliances to be used. See the Load Chart and Planning Worksheet in the Appendix.

The Load chart lists typical amp draws of most electrical equipment. Next enter how many hours each piece of equipment typically is in use during a day. Multiply the amps for each piece of equipment times the total hours it is used to get the total amp hours for each piece of equipment. Then calculate the projected amp-hour total for the period of time the system will run on batteries in between charges. This is usually six to 12 hours. Add an additional 25 percent to the amp-hour total as a safety margin and thus you have the total amp-hour requirements for the battery bank.

Next determine the approximate usable amp hour capacity of your battery. You cannot use the entire amp hour rating of your battery. Multiply the battery's amp hour rating by 50 percent for an older battery, or by 75 percent for a newer battery. Divide this figure by the total amp hour usage. The result is the approximate number of hours you can draw power off the battery bank without having to recharge. Drawing electrical power without recharging after this point may damage the battery and possibly some of the electrical equipment too.

In order to determine how long it will take to recharge your batteries, consider the size of the battery bank, the output of the generator, alternator or battery charger, and how low the charge is in the battery. In theory, a 50-amp battery charger can charge 50 amp-hours of power every hour. Thus, if the system used 100 amps out of the battery bank since the last charge, the generator powering the 50 amps battery charger will have to run for two hours in order to bring the batteries back up to full charge. This is not fully accurate since batteries are not 100 percent efficient. In reality, the batteries have 35 percent resistance to charging unless they are the newer glass mat batteries. A conventional lead acid battery charges more slowly as the battery charge is topped off.

Battery chargers also have an amp rating. This rating determines how many amps the charger will put into your battery bank each hour without consideration for the battery's resistance.

Installation

Batteries require careful installation for safety and longevity. They should be accessible and fastened down with heavy nylon straps to keep them stable in the event of an earthquake. Conventional lead acid batteries need to be housed in compartments with ventilated covers that allow the explosive hydrogen gas to be evacuated. The ventilation of the battery compartment is necessary to protect the batteries from excessive heat, which reduces battery performance and life. This ventilation should be positive pressure so that the explosive hydrogen gas is not pulled through a ventilation blower, but the air under pressure is pushed into the battery compartment and the hydrogen gas is forced out by positive pressure. One venting option is a Hydro Cap, which converts hydrogen back into water and puts that water back into the battery.

Read the manufacturer's instructions before installation and call the customer support number with any questions, or consult with an experienced installer.

Maintenance

Batteries should be kept clean by wiping them with a disposable rag. Clean the battery terminals and cable ends with a wire brush and baking soda and water at least once a year. Get terminal protector spray from an auto parts store and treat the posts and cable ends once they are clean.

Check the water level in the cells once a week. Top off battery cells with distilled water only to the level of the split ring or other internal mark. If you are constantly adding large amounts of water to all the cells, the batteries are probably being overcharged. If you have to constantly add water to just one cell, then that cell is probably dead and the battery needs to be replaced.

Charging

Batteries should be kept fully charged when not in use. The charge can be checked with a voltmeter or cell hydrometer. At full charge with the generator off, the voltmeter should read 12.5 volts. A reading of 11 volts means the battery is below full charge. Test each cell for specific gravity with a hydrometer. A reading of 1.26 to 1.28 indicates a full charge. A reading of 1.20 indicates a cell is not fully charged.

Charge the batteries by running the generator or battery charger. A slow charge will give a conventional lead acid battery a fuller charge than a fast charge. A glass mat battery can be charged quickly.

Self-Discharge

All lead acid batteries left to stand will slowly lose charge. This is referred to as self-discharge. Batteries require maintenance and recharging or they will eventually go flat and be ruined.

When the system is not in use, a trickle charge makes up for self-discharge. Check every 60 days or so and recharge as necessary.

Freezing can damage batteries. Try to keep them in a place that will not freeze. A fully charged battery has greater resistance to freezing.

The switch panel, terminal block, and wires should be both accessible and protected.

Cycling: Deep vs. Shallow and Depth of Discharge

Rechargeable batteries absorb and give up electricity by a reversible electrochemical reaction. A battery storage power system requires rechargeable deep-cycle batteries that can stand repeated cycles of deep discharge. A cycle means to discharge then recharge.

If a battery is discharged beyond the optimum point, its life span will be shortened. If it is discharged completely and left uncharged, the battery will be ruined.

Batteries are designed to endure at a given number of charge-discharge cycles at a specific depth of discharge. This Depth of Discharge (DOD) rating indicates the predictable battery life span in terms of total charge/discharge cycles. The DOD is the optimum amount that the battery can be discharged without shortening the battery's life.

How deep a battery is discharged is termed depth of discharge. Battery manufacturers provide depth of discharge ratings, usually determined at either 50 or 30 percent, or both.

A shallow cycle occurs when only the top 20 percent or less of the battery's power is discharged and then recharged. Some batteries, like automotive starting batteries, are designed for this type of cycling only. The plates of active material are thin with large overall surface area. This design can give up lots of power in a very short time.

On the other hand, a deep cycle battery typically discharges 80 percent of capacity before recharging. They have a thicker plate of active material with less overall surface area. Because of the lesser surface area available for chemical reaction, they yield just as much power relative to their size, but do so over a longer period of time. This type of battery design is preferred for a solar photovoltaic system because discharging a battery to a deeper level is normal during extended cloudy weather.

The depth of cycling has a good deal to do with determining a battery's useful life. Even batteries designed for deep cycling are "used up" faster as the depth of discharge is increased. It is common practice for a system to be designed with deep cycle batteries even though the daily or average discharging only goes to a relatively shallow depth. Shallow cycle your deep cycle battery for the most cycles.

Temperature Effects

Conventional lead acid batteries provide power based on a chemical reaction. The optimum operating temperature for a lead-acid battery is 77 degrees Fahrenheit. The warmer the temperature, the faster the rate. The colder the temperature, the slower the reaction rate.

Most people have experienced this effect when they tried to start the car on a sub-zero morning and their battery doesn't produce enough electricity to start the engine.

Conventional lead acid batteries should be stored in a temperature-controlled environment between 55 and 80 degrees. If the batteries are installed in an area exposed to cold temperatures, the battery capacity must be increased to compensate for this derating. High temperatures also shorten the life of the battery.

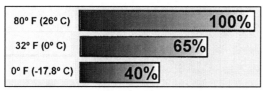

Comparison of cranking power available from fully charged conventional lead acid battery at various temperatures

Cold Cranking Amps

Cold Cranking Amps is a term used to classify car batteries. Car batteries have no application in alternative battery storage systems because they are not capable of deep cycling, which is a primary requirement. A Cold Cranking Amp rating indicates a shallow cycling battery.

Sulfation

Sulfation is a natural by-product of battery operation and is the major cause of shortened battery lifespan. With each charge and discharge cycle a small amount of lead sulfate coating accumulates on the interior plates. Batteries that are run fully flat or drawn down below their rated safe depth of discharge will accumulate lead sulfate coatings at an accelerated pace. Sulfation buildup occurs when sulfur molecules in the battery acid discharge to the point where they crystallize and coat the battery's lead plates. The more the plates are coated, the less energy they will accept or release. Before long they become so coated the battery dies.

If the lead sulfate build-up on the battery plates can be reduced, then

Battery Amp-Hour Capacity and Deep Cycle Comparison

Battery Type	Amp. Hr. Capacity	Tolerated Deep Cycles
Auto - 12 volt	60 - 70	20
R.V. - 12 volt	100	200
Golf Cart - 6 volt	20	250
Mining Vehicle - 6 volt	350	750
Glass Mat - 12 volt	255	1100

the life of the battery can be extended.

A number of companies manufacture electronic devices that are purported to reduce sulfation. These devices emit pulsating DC current that re-energizes the crystallized sulfates that have accumulated on the battery plates. This process removes the lead sulfate coating from the plates and puts it back into the sulfuric acid battery electrolyte as active sulfur molecules. The U.S. military, some municipalities and truck fleets have started using these devices. The other value of this type of device is that they are also float or trickle chargers. Manufacturers claim that these devices can extend battery life up to 5 times their rated life span.

Pulse Tech Products Corporation makes the PowerPulse battery maintenance system. PowerPulse is an electronic device that actually uses voltage to eliminate sulfation and related problems.

Battery Types

Lead-Antimony

There are three types of lead acid batteries, but only the lead-antimony is appropriate for home or shelter power systems. Lead-antimony batteries have high discharge rates, good charge/discharge efficiencies and high reliability in fast charging and deep cycling use. This type of battery is especially appropriate for systems with generators and battery chargers.

Lead acid batteries can be obtained in the conventional flooded type or in the sealed-gelled type. A flooded type uses a liquid sulfuric acid electrolyte, and the sealed-gelled type uses a fully gelled electrolyte. The advantage of the sealed-gelled battery is low maintenance. However, they cost about 35 percent more than the conventional flooded type.

Nickel-Cadmium

Nickel-cadmium batteries have many advantages over the lead acid battery. One hundred percent of the stored power in a Ni-Cad can be used without seriously harming the battery and it can be left for years at a partial or depleted state of charge without causing severe damage. Low temperature does not affect the performance of the nickel-cadmium battery. These batteries can last 20 or more years. Ni-Cads achieve the longest life when they are cycled no lower than 20 percent below their total capacity. Nickel-Cadmium batteries cost six to ten times more than a comparable lead acid battery.

Avoid inexpensive used nickel-cadmium batteries. Because of the cadmium, Ni-Cad batteries have to be disposed of at a licensed toxic waste disposal site. There aren't many of these locations in the U.S. that provide this service, and those that do will charge a hefty price.

There is also a new variation of the Ni-Cad called a Fiber-nickel-cadmium that has an internal fiber system instead of conventional plates. The rated life span for this new Ni-Cad is 15,000 cycles at a 25 percent depth of discharge.

Surplus Lead-Calcium

From time to time the telephone companies retire Lead-Calcium batteries that they used to backup their systems. These batteries are usually relatively inexpensive and normally have a lot of life left in them, but they have certain drawbacks. Lead-Calcium batteries don't like to be cycled below 15 percent of their capacity. Also the cells are four to five times larger than the cells of a comparable lead-acid battery. This means they take up more room and they are harder to move.

Nickel-Iron

Nickel-iron batteries were made by the Edison company years ago. These batteries were mainly used as locomotive batteries. They lasted 50 years or longer. This is probably the reason that no one in the U.S. makes them any more. There is no profit in a battery that lasts forever. Used nickel iron batteries occasionally can be found if you scrounge around.

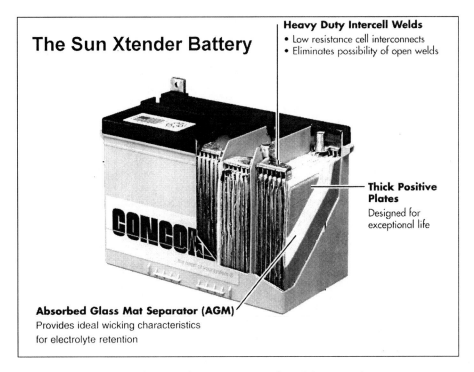

The Sun Xtender Battery

Heavy Duty Intercell Welds
• Low resistance cell interconnects
• Eliminates possibility of open welds

Thick Positive Plates
Designed for exceptional life

Absorbed Glass Mat Separator (AGM)
Provides ideal wicking characteristics for electrolyte retention

Absorbent Glass Mat Lead Acid Batteries

The absorbent glass mat lead acid battery is a recent innovation. This battery is the first significant improvement in battery technology to come on the market in the past 20 years. Concord manufactures the Sun Xtender. They have about 30 percent more life than a conventional lead acid industrial deep-cycle battery.

At a 50 percent depth of discharge, the Sun Xtender glass mat battery provides up to 1000 cycles; at a 30 percent depth of discharge it gets up to 1800 cycles. A good conventional industrial lead acid battery has a life expectancy of about 700 cycles at 50 percent depth of discharge.

Glass mat batteries are the most efficient batteries on the market today. Unlike conventional Gel-Cell batteries, fast charging does not damage glass mat batteries. Fast charging is the leading cause of gel-cell battery failure. Glass mat batteries have very little resistance to charging—only about 5 percent resistance compared to 35 percent inefficiency for a conventional industrial lead acid battery.

Glass mat batteries perform well at cold temperatures. They operate efficiently between - 40° F and 160° F. One of the unique characteristics of glass mat batteries is that they have very little self-discharge—only one percent per month, compared to 20 percent monthly for conventional lead acid batteries. Self-discharge is the leading cause of conventional lead acid battery failure.

Glass mat batteries have cells sealed with pressure relief valves that confine any gases produced during cell operation. These gases are then recombined back into water, eliminating the loss of water from the cells and the need for water replenishment.

The glass mat battery differs significantly from the conventional gelled electrolyte battery, or gel-cell. The electrolyte in conventional gel-cell batteries consists of a mixture of finely divided silica or sand mixed with a sulfuric acid solution. This gelled electrolyte is highly viscous. During charge and discharge it often develops voids or cracks that impede acid flow and result in loss of battery capacity. As these voids increase, more and more plate area is left dry and unable to provide a path for ionic flow, thus progressively reducing battery capacity.

Glass mat batteries are maintenance-free. If they tip over, they will not leak acid. Glass mat batteries do not require equalization and should not be put through an equalizing charge. They should never be charged at a higher voltage, which causes prolonged gassing.

Final Battery Considerations

It is not a good idea to mix batteries of differing type and age. This tends to shorten the life of the battery bank.

One final consideration regarding batteries is the dry storage of spare batteries for future use, keeping the liquid electrolyte separate. This is a very good idea but requires care. Not all batteries are manufactured with a truly dry method. Even though you can purchase most batteries special order without the electrolyte in them, the lead plates will still sulfate and ruin during dry storage if the battery was not manufactured with a truly dry process.

Batteries in Parallel vs. Series

Batteries may be wired in either series or parallel configuration. When wired in series, the positive terminal is wired to the next battery's negative terminal. This increases the voltage while maintaining the amperage of the two batteries. With parallel wiring, the positive terminal is wired to the next battery's positive terminal, and the negative terminals are wired. This increases amperage while maintaining voltage.

A battery bank may combine both series and parallel wiring configurations. Batteries are usually wired in series in order to achieve a specific voltage. A number of batteries wired in series can be connected together in parallel to increase the amp hour capacity of a given battery bank. One disadvantage to having batteries in parallel is that if one has a bad cell, it will pull down the performance of the entire bank. This is not the case with batteries wired in series.

Fuse Panel

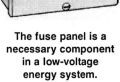

The arteries of a low-voltage electrical system—the wires that take power to the appliances—first go through a fuse panel or circuit breaker panel. The drawing shows a typical circuit with a 4-breaker switch panel and fuses.

The fuse panel is a necessary component in a low-voltage energy system.

What Size Wire?

Consider the installation of a water pump rated at 12 amps. The wire run from the switch panel to the water tank is fourteen feet, requiring 14 feet of wire (one positive and one negative conductor). To prevent overheating and voltage loss, choose the proper wire size by referring to the Appendix Wire Size Table. Rounding off the pump amperage to 10 and the wire run to 15, we find 14-gauge wire, which will deliver the necessary power with minimum resistance loss. Always use wire rated for marine service, which is both moisture and heat resistant. Use braided copper-stranded wire, not solid core wire.

DC Battery Chargers

A diesel powered DC battery charger is one option for small to medium-sized systems. They have been used for years in the marine industry. Balmar makes one in both 12- and 24-volt configurations. Models vary in capacity from 75 to 200 amps. The Balmar PC-75 is powered by a water-cooled 4 HP Kubota diesel that will produce 70 amps of 12-volt DC power continuously for 24 hours using only three gallons of #2 diesel fuel. Most Balmar units are diesel powered with either a Yanmar or a Kubota engine. Balmar units with water-cooled engines can be ordered with marine heat exchangers.

Maintenance

A scheduled maintenance program is absolutely necessary for anyone using generators to produce power. This means not just during an actual emergency power failure, but especially keeping systems maintained and ready for use prior to an emergency. It is too easy to let valuable equipment and systems go into decay and neglect.

Power Generation and Water Pumping

Pumping water from wells is one of the most challenging electrical loads for independent power systems. Conventional well pumps are usually powered by 220 volt AC. In a conventional well water system, when the pressure switch senses that the water pressure in the system has dropped below a certain pre-determined level it switches on power to the well pump. Well systems also incorporate a pressure tank that has a rubber balloon-like bladder that inflates when the well pump is turned on. This inflated bladder creates a reserve of water pressure in the system. If the water system did not have a pressure tank, the well pump would automatically turn on when anyone opened a faucet.

It is not practical to keep a fuel-powered generator running 24 hours a day, waiting to meet the electrical demand when the well pump decides to turn on. It is better to store water in a reserve tank than to store electrical power in a battery bank for running the pump as water is needed.

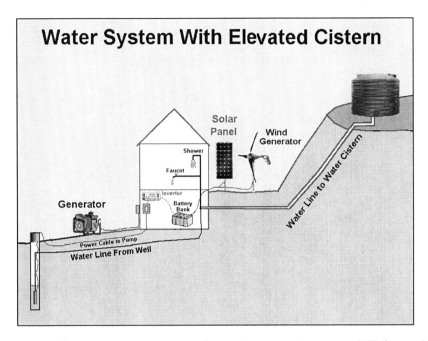

One solution is to create an elevated water cistern, uphill from the house. In a situation where the generator is running for one or two hours in the morning and evening, the well pump would be turned on and used to fill the elevated water cistern. When the generator was turned off, the elevated water cistern would provide gravity fed water. The pressure of this water would vary according to the size of the tank and how high it was elevated. You can flush the toilet and have running water coming out of the tap with as little as 5 psi. A good shower could take 20 psi or more.

Companies that make concrete septic tanks also usually make concrete water storage tanks. These tanks are designed to be buried. In colder climates, burying a tank in the ground protects the water in the tank from freezing. Starting out with a larger diameter pipe and reducing the pipe in size as it travels downhill to the house will help increase the final water pressure in the house.

In the event that the home site location does not have sufficient rise to accommodate an elevated water cistern, another workable option is to place a water cistern close to the house and use a low voltage DC booster pump to maintain pressure on demand. This is the same type of system that is used in recreational vehicles to provide water pressure. Like the elevated cistern

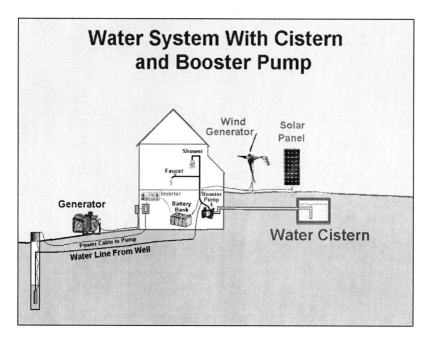

option, a fuel powered generator powers the well pump that fills the water cistern once a day, but when the generator is turned off, water pressure is provided on demand by a battery powered low-voltage booster pump.

Another option is to go with a low-voltage well pumping system. This system works best with one of the water cistern options explained above. This well pumping system is typically powered by solar electric panels or a wind generator. It runs continuously and gradually fills the tank. Another option is to use a low-voltage pump in conjunction with a battery bank, a pressure tank and pressure switch as explained above.

There is a special type of 220-volt AC submersible pump that is non-surging. The brand name of this product is "Jet Sub." As we have previously discussed, standard AC pumps can draw three to four times the normal operating current while starting. The Jet Sub pump has a soft start. This pump takes four seconds for the pump motor to wind up to full speed. This results in a more constant power draw and a reduced surge. Consequently, an inverter for this type of pump does not have to be as big, and the inverter is less apt to be drawn down below its capacity in the event that other loads are running when the pump decides to kick on. This pump requires a true sine wave inverter in combination with a 220-volt transformer since 117

VAC inverters don't produce 220 volts.

Standard 220-volt AC $^1/_3$ to $^1/_2$ horsepower submersible pumps pump a more substantial volume of water per minute. Thus, when a cistern is being filled, these pumps do not have to operate as long as a non-surging or a low-voltage pump. When using a standard AC pump, a properly sized inverter is critical. Typically, two of the household's largest loads, the well pump and the washing machine, are usually operated together at the same time. The inverter and batteries need to be sized to accommodate their combined surge demand.

Pressure Increase for Elevated Water Tanks Feet of Elevation	P.S.I. Water Pressure
136	60
115	50
92	40
69	30
46	20
23	10

For shallower well applications, submersible $^1/_3$ and $^1/_2$ HP 110-volt AC pumps will operate from power produced by a 117-volt AC modified sine wave inverter. These surging pumps do not require a transformer since they are 110-volt AC, but their minimal horsepower limits their use.

Electrical Terms

Certain terms are used to measure the quantity and force of electrical power. The similarities in the flow of water and electricity can help us understand amperes and volts. Electrical power (the ability to do work) is a function of pressure (voltage) and amount or volume (amperage). Double either and you double the power the current carries through the circuit.

Amperage

Amperage represents volume of the electrical current. Amperes, or amps, represent the rate of flow, like the volume or gallons per minute of flowing water.

Ammeter

An ammeter measures the flow of electric current. This instrument measures electrical gallons per minute. It is placed in series in the electrical circuit that senses electrical flow magnetically and registers amperage on a dial. In a power generating system, an ammeter is placed on the cable coming out of the alternator or generator. This meter shows the amount of current flowing out of the generator or alternator. For example, in a DC low-voltage system, if the ammeter reads 20, this is an indication that the alternator is putting out 20 amps. This electrical power will either charge the battery or be used by electrical appliances on the line. If the ammeter reads 0 and no appliances are in use, then either the battery is fully charged and not accepting any further charge or the alternator has failed.

Volts

Voltage represents the electrical current strength. Volts represent the force of electricity similar to the pressure of water in a pipe or the pounds per square inch.

Voltmeter

A voltmeter is a gauge that measures electrical pressure. The voltage, or force of the current, is measured by a voltmeter, an instrument placed parallel in the circuit. When the generator engine is running, the voltage produced by the alternator in a 12-volt system is actually about 13.5 volts. A fully charged battery produces a voltage of about 12.5 volts. When the voltmeter drops below 11 volts, the battery has lost its usable charge.

Watts

The watt is the basic unit of measure for determining the size of electrical loads. Light fixtures and electrical appliances are rated in terms of watts. Watt is a measurement of electrical power that takes into consideration both the volts and the amps used by an appliance. If you multiply the volts an appliance uses by the amps it draws, the result will equal the total wattage.

Formula: Watts = Volts x Amperes

If we had a 100-watt appliance running on 24 volts, this would mean the appliance would draw 4.16 amperes. Or, if we had a 12-volt appliance that draws 15 amperes then we have a 180-watt electrical load.

Watt-hour

A watt-hour is a measure of power consumption. One watt-hour equals a 1-watt load that is powered for one hour. A 100-watt load powered for two hours will consume 200 watt-hours.

Amperehours

An amperehour is a measure of the volume of electrical power used by an appliance in an hour's time. One amperehour equals a one-ampere load that is powered for one hour. If a 120-volt, 100-watt unit is run for one hour it will consume .83 amperehours.

Kilowatts

A kilowatt (kW) equals 1000 watts.
Formula: Watts/1000 = kilowatts. Example: 3000 watts/1000 = 3 kW.

Kilowatt-hour

A kilowatt-hour is a measure of the power of electricity in thousand watts used by an appliance in an hour's time. One kilowatt-hour equals a 1-kilowatt load that is powered for one hour. A one kilowatt-hour could result from a 100-watt load being powered for 10 hours or a 1000-watt load being powered for one hour.

Electricity is the flow of electrons. The nature of electricity is analogous to the flow of water from an elevated storage tank through pipes into a turbine. When the outlet control valve on the water tank is opened, the water flows downhill with a hydraulic head pressure that is the product of the difference between the water storage tank elevation and the elevation of the lower of the discharge outlets. The higher the elevation of the water tank, the higher the hydraulic pressure will be at the lower discharge point. The greater the volume of water in the elevated tank, the greater the pressure at the lower discharge point.

One factor that reduces this hydraulic head pressure is friction in the pipes and the friction created as the water forces its way through the turbine. In an electrical circuit, the battery is the elevated tank that stores electrons. When the switch is turned on, electrons flow out of the battery through the wires.

Just like the volume of water, the voltage of the battery determines the pressure of the electron flow. The higher the battery voltage bank, the greater the pressure or flow of current in the wire distribution system. In the same way as water, electron flow pressure is reduced by friction in the wires and the use of electrons by appliances on the line, such as lights or motors.

As the volume of water drains from the tank, the water pressure drops at the lower discharge point, and the volume of water flow decreases in terms of gallons per minute. Similarly, as the battery's stored electrical energy is used, the volts in the distribution line drops and the volume of electrical energy or amperage drops.

Resistance and Ohms

Friction created by appliances and wires is called resistance and is measured in ohms. Thus, the rate of current flow (amperes) is a product of the voltage reduced by the resistance. This relationship is the basis of Ohm's Law.

Ohm's Law

Ohm's Law states that electrical current or amperage equals voltage divided by resistance. This formula A = V/R can be used to determine any unknown factor if any two of the three factors are known. If we increase the voltage by adding an additional battery in series, the current will also increase. If we add more resistance in the form of appliances, the current or amperage will decrease. If more current (amperage) is needed to operate the system, then either the voltage will have to be increased or the resistance (the appliances) will have to be decreased.

Components of a Hybrid Independent Electrical Power System

Component	Function
Fuel Powered Generator	Provides backup AC power and power for heavy AC loads
Hydroelectric Generator	Generates DC electrical power from hydro
Wind Powered Generator	Generates DC electrical power from wind
Solar Panel Modules	Collects sunlight and produces DC electrical power
Controller	Regulates power to and from batteries
Fusing/Breakers	Overcurrent protection for wires and appliances
Battery bank	Stores DC electrical power
Monitors and meters	Gives readout of the system status and power flows
Inverter	Changes low voltage DC power to high voltage AC power
Battery Charger	Converts AC (generator power) to DC
Fuel tank	Provides reserve fuel supply for fuel-powered generator

CHAPTER 13
Medical Considerations

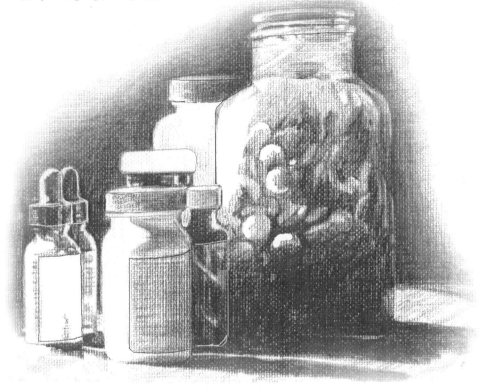

It is inevitable that during or after a crisis, traumatic injuries and medical emergencies will occur. The nature of the disaster will limit the availability of conventional medical services. The extent to which medical services will be available will depend on the scope and severity of the disaster.

Hence medical preparations are critical. The extent to which one can provide medical services is going to be proportionate to the level of training acquired and the available equipment.

Many of the routine injuries and emergencies that normally are successfully treated will move into a critical category. For example, the general health of the population will be weakened due to breakdowns in sanitation and malnutrition caused by food shortages. Malnutrition weakens the body's immune system that increases susceptibility to uncontrolled infections. If the disaster is nuclear, immune systems will be further suppressed by exposure to dangerous levels of radiation.

Triage, the sorting of patients, will become a more common practice. When medical resources are limited, sorting concentrates available resources on the most salvageable patients.

Allopathic Considerations

Pre-hospital Care

For the sake of preparedness it would be good to get some training in pre-hospital care. There are a number of levels to what is called pre-hospital care. The first level is standard first aid (eight-hour course). The next level is called first responder (46-hour course), then emergency medical technician (EMT, 120-hour course) and finally paramedic (one year of training).

Every prepared individual needs to know the basics of patient assessment. Patient assessment involves checking a person's vital signs. When a serious injury or condition occurs, the body automatically makes an attempt to compensate for the problem or deficiency. Any sign of this irregular compensation effort indicates the presence of a problem in the body.

Blood carries oxygen and nutrition to the vital organs and all of the living tissue of the body. When a blood shortage occurs in the circulatory system and body parts receive inadequate oxygen supplies, the brain gets signals from different parts of the body that pressure is dropping due to a lack of fluid volume.

The first thing the brain does is to try to compensate for the problem by constricting all of the blood vessels, which reduces the overall volume of the vascular system. This keeps the plumbing system full by reducing its size and the reduced blood volume is initially able to meet the basic demand functions of the vital organs. This is what is referred to as compensated shock. If the problem persists, be it dehydration or bleeding, and the blood volume continues to decrease, then the brain shifts into "Plan B."

Once the brain has exhausted its capacity to compensate by reducing the size and volume of the vascular system, then all it can do is turn up the speed of the central pump, the heart. Speeding up the pump moves the reduced volume of blood at a faster rate, temporarily servicing the demands of the vital organs. Since the lungs oxygenate the blood and work in sync with the heart, the breathing rate increases. So an increase in the heart rate, or pulse, and the respiration are the first two signs of de-compensated shock. The third sign is the actual reduction of pressure in the vascular system.

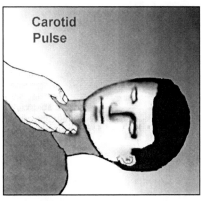

The pulse can be most easily felt where the larger arteries are near the skin.

Check the pulse rate by pressing a finger on a vein, like the jugular (neck), the brachial (upper arm) or radial (wrist) artery. Or listen to the heartbeat with a stethoscope. Measure blood pressure with a stethoscope and a blood pressure cuff.

Oxygen is the most powerful drug available for basic life support. Medical-grade oxygen works wonders on patients suffering from shock and numerous medical complications. Unless the patient has a history of chronic obstructive pulmonary disease (COPD), you cannot overdose them with oxygen. An EMT book will give full instruction on the administration of oxygen. An adult suffering from severe trauma or shock should receive eight to 15 liters of oxygen per minute via a non-re-breather mask. If the patient's condition is not critical or oxygen is in short supply, oxygen can be administered via a nasal cannula at rates of one to six liters per minute.

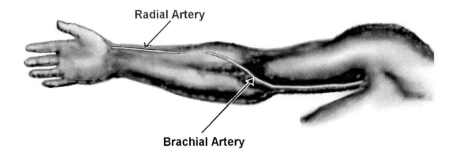

Radial Artery

Brachial Artery

Administering oxygen to patients is almost always beneficial.

Oxygen therapy uses up compressed oxygen fairly quickly. For this reason the use of oxygen may be restricted unless you can stockpile a quantity of "H" size cylinders. A small "D" cylinder will last about 28 minutes when being discharged at a rate of ten liters per minute and an "H" cylinder will last about 9.5 hours when being discharged at the same rate. You will need the appropriate regulator to use the oxygen out of a cylinder and the large "H" cylinder will require a flow-meter.

Like any other compressed gas cylinder, oxygen bottles need to be secured in position with adequate clamps or brackets. If a bottle tips over and breaks off the exposed regulator, the cylinder becomes a torpedo-like projectile that has the capacity to pass through masonry walls.

It is not within the scope of this book to adequately cover pre-hospital care. Also, just reading a book is not good enough. A person needs to get training and hands-on practice.

Beyond Pre-hospital Care

All of this pre-hospital training is valuable, but in a major disaster we are talking about a situation where there is not a hospital to take the patient to. The situation could involve the actual treatment of the patient. The only person certified to do this is the doctor. But if it means the patient dies or you try, it is much better that you try!

Two excellent books help prepare for medical emergencies during a disaster. One is *Where There Is No Doctor, a Village Health Care Handbook,* by David Werner, and the other is *Ditch Medicine,* by Hugh L. Coffee. Both of these books are written for unskilled personnel. *Where There Is No Doctor* deals with instruction geared toward improvising medical services in remote third world situations. This is exactly the type of environment we might find ourselves in during a war or a major national disaster. *Ditch Medicine* picks up when *Where There Is No Doctor* leaves off. This book deals with serious trauma, gunshot wounds, intravenous therapy, surgery and more. *Where There is No Doctor* is available through Yellowstone Trading.

Vital Signs

Age	Weight (Pounds)	Pulse	Respirations	Blood Pressure Systolic	Diastolic
Newborn (0 – 2 mo.)	5.5 – 8.8	94 – 145	30 – 60	60 – 90	
Infants (2 – 12 mo.)	8.8 – 22	124 – 170	30 – 60	74 – 100	
Toddlers (1 – 3 yrs.)	22 – 33	98 – 160	24 – 40	80 – 112	
Preschool (4 – 5 yrs.)	33 – 44	66 – 132	22 – 34	82 – 110	
School Age (6 – 12 yrs.)	44 – 88	70 – 110	18 – 30	84 – 120	
Adolescent (12+ yrs.)	over 88	55 – 105	12 – 16	94 – 140	
Adult		60 – 80	12 – 20	90 –180	60 – 104

Blood Sugar Levels: Low = less than 60, Normal = 70 to 180, High = above 240

Note: Due to the fact that circulatory systems of children and adolescents have a great ability to compensate for shock (blood volume loss), any sign of drop in blood pressure for children and adolescents indicates a critical situation. When adults start going into shock, the vital signs will generally show a gradual drop in blood pressure and a corresponding increase in respirations and pulse rate. When the circulatory system of a child or adolescent exceeds its capacity to compensate for blood loss through constriction of the blood vessels, an immediate crash of vital signs occurs. This usually happens so rapidly that the patient does not survive without immediate intervention of advanced life support. Dehydration can also cause shock. The best indicator of shock in children and adolescents is the appearance of delayed capillary refill. Capillary refill can be observed by pressing your finger against the fingernail bed, or the leg of an infant. Once you remove your finger after firmly pressing for about four seconds, the area should look lighter in color than the surrounding area due to a lack of blood in the tissue. In a healthy person, this lighter colored tissue should return to its pinkish color within two seconds. This is called capillary refill. If it takes much longer than two seconds, you may have a serious problem—compensated shock. Treat the patient immediately for shock and obtain the best available medical treatment as soon as possible. Other signs that indicate the onset of shock in infants and children include pale skin color, a blue color to hands and feet and the presence of a lethargic or altered state of consciousness.

Bacterial vs. Viral

There are basically two different causes of most common diseases, bacteria and viruses. Determining the cause of a disease will help in determining how to cure it.

Bacterial

Illnesses caused by bacteria will very often respond to antibiotics. Some of the most common include strep throat, bronchitis and ear infections. Another not quite so common but very serious illness that responds to antibiotic treatment is Giardia, a bacterial infection contracted through drinking contaminated water. Anthrax, Bubonic and Pneumonic Plague, Staph, E-coli, Brucellosis, Cholera, Tularemia and Q Fever are caused by bacterial agents. Some of these illnesses are contagious.

Where There is No Doctor **is extremely helpful when professional medical help is not available. It is comprehensive yet simple to understand.**

Where There Is No Doctor contains a comprehensive list of antibiotics, the diseases they treat, doses, administration, precautions and side effects.

Antibiotics could be in high demand and short supply during a major disaster and so could be extremely expensive and a highly valued barter items.

Antibiotics are best used as a last resort in a life-threatening situation involving an uncontrolled bacterial infection. Antibiotics should not be used on infections that the body's own immune function can successfully contain. There are several reasons for this. Some people will have serious allergic reactions to the antibiotic. Antibiotics also tend to kill beneficial bacteria in the intestines. With repeated use of antibiotics, resistant strains of bacteria can develop.

It is difficult to obtain and stockpile prescription medications without a prescription. This can be overcome by purchasing through the mail from foreign sources. The U.S. Postal Service, the FDA and U.S. Customs are not obstructing small shipments of prescription drugs mailed into the country from foreign suppliers to American residents. Here are sources for ordering prescription drugs over the Internet from Mexico:

www.eprescribe.com

www.safewebmedical.com

www.medprescribe.com

The acquisition of veterinary drugs is another legal option. Many of the antibiotics used for humans are also used for livestock. Do not order an antibiotic that is not listed for use in *Where There Is No Doctor*. For those with advanced life support skills, these veterinary supply houses also sell epinephrine.

Jeffers Vet Supply is a source of mail order veterinary drugs. A local agricultural/farm supply store will sell a lesser variety of drugs over the counter.

Natural antibiotic alternatives include Golden Seal, Garlic and Echinacea. Less well known are lobelia, grapefruit seed concentrate, colloidal silver and a line of German homeopathic antibiotics manufactured by Sanum-Kehlbeck. We can personally attest to the effectiveness of the Sanum remedies. One reliable source for herbal supplements that work is Dr. Richard Schulze. To order his products, including videos and tapes on how to use them, visit his web site, www.dr-schulze.com.

Viruses

Illness caused by viruses will not respond to antibiotics. The medical profession has very little to offer when faced with a viral illness. The common cold and the flu are two well-known viral illnesses. Others include smallpox, encephalitis, and hemorrhagic fevers. Viruses are definitely contagious.

Anti-viral herbs used by native cultures include olive leaf extract, oil of oregano and elderberry. Detailed information is available on the Internet.

Olive Leaf Extract – This herb has been used for severe cases of fever and malaria for more than 150 years. In the late 1960s, a major American pharmaceutical company, Upjohn, conducted scientific research on elenolic acid, the active ingredient in oleuropein, a substance found in olive leaf, which was effective against every virus it was tested on, including retrovirus, bacterium or protozoan such as influenza, the common cold, meningitis, encephalitis, herpes, chronic fatigue and hepatitis.

Oregano – Oregano oil has been tested against a variety of microorganisms and found to be anti-fungal, anti-parasitic, anti-viral and antibacterial, according to *The Cure Is in the Cupboard: How to Use Oregano for Better Health* by Dr. Cass Ingram. Researchers in Mexico found it to be effective against Giardia. It has been used to treat hard-to-handle chronic problems such as Shingles, Candida, Reflux disease, chronic arthritis, fungus and other infections. In an article published in Phytotherapy Research, oil of oregano is described as superseding anti-inflammatory drugs in reversing pain and inflammation and being nearly as powerful as morphine as a painkiller. Oregano must be of the wild variety (high mountain variety) and not commercial oregano, which is often Mexican sage.

Oregano

One of our readers reported she used oil of oregano to successfully ward off Legionnaire's disease. She was on a long airplane trip to Hawaii with her husband. At the onset of the flight she and her husband started feeling sick. She also noticed other passengers exhibiting the same symptoms, so she took four drops of oil of oregano under her tongue every two hours throughout the flight, but her husband did not. Her husband was very sick by the end of the flight and ended up staying in bed during most of their nine-day stay in Hawaii. She continued using the oil of oregano. Upon returning home, the husband went to his family doctor and had a blood test done. It came out positive for Legionnaire's disease. He underwent a successful treatment with high potency antibiotics. She did not contract Legionnaire's disease.

One easy way to take oil of oregano is to put four to five drops in a gelatin capsule and swallow it.

Elderberry – The berries of elderberry have been used in early folk medicine to treat influenza. World-renowned virologist Dr. Madeleine

Mumcuoglu has done extensive testing with elderberry with Southern Israel flu epidemic patients of 1992–93. Within 24 hours, 20 percent of those patients taking the elderberry had dramatic improvements in their flu symptoms. By the second day, 73 percent were improved and by the third day, 90 percent. In the control group, only 16 percent felt better after two days and the majority of that group took almost a week to begin feeling better.

Elderberry

Since viruses can have such a debilitating effect on one's health, it makes sense to look into these possible cures. Don't wait until there is a disaster to find out that the medical profession isn't able to help you.

Painkillers and Anesthesia

Painkillers and anesthesia will be hard to get in a disaster. Non-prescription analgesics (pain-killers) such as aspirin (acetylsalic acid) and Tylenol (acetaminophen) can easily be stockpiled. Codeine is the next level of painkiller, but obtainable only with a prescription. Lidocaine (Xylocaine, a local injectable painkiller that requires a prescription) is used to deaden pain before suturing a wound. Morphine is the top of the line painkiller for serious trauma. Morphine is a wonder drug when it comes to shock, pain suppression and other medical emergencies, but it is highly controlled because of illicit use. Unfortunately, no legal vehicle exists for the obtaining it for disasters.

Modern anesthesia is too high-tech and expensive for most disaster preparedness programs and requires highly skilled personnel. The old-fashioned anesthesia was ethyl ether. This is not the stuff you start your diesel truck with when it is cold outside. Squibb makes this in 1/4 lb. copper-lined cans. If your group has the expertise and equipment to perform surgical procedures, ethyl ether should be in your medical kit.

Ethyl ether can be dripped onto a cloth over the person's nose and mouth to facilitate the inhalation of this anesthesia. The fabric covering the nose and mouth should permit the free passage of air and anesthetic vapor and the unobstructed elimination of carbon dioxide. This fabric covering can be made of 8 to 12 layers of surgical sponge gauze.

Ethyl ether is highly flammable and overdoses can cause respiratory arrest. The overdose antidote is artificial respiration and the administering of oxygen or fresh air.

All drugs sold in the United States have expiration dates. Expiration dates are conservative estimates of the date at which the drug's stated potency, as listed on the label, can no longer be guaranteed. This does not mean that after this date the drug becomes toxic. It does mean that a pre-scribed dosage might not work due to degeneration in the drug's potency.

There are three factors to consider when storing perishable items. These are temperature, sunlight and humidity. If the drugs are in a dry capsule form, try to keep them in a freezer or refrigerator. Ultraviolet ray (sunlight) exposure tends to degenerate many products. Keep it out of sunlight. High moisture contributes to degeneration. Medications in sealed, tamperproof containers probably will not be affected by humidity, but medications in powdered forms should be carefully repackaged in airtight containers.

Naturopathic Considerations

Natural measures help maintain health and improve the body's immune resistance. In extreme life-threatening situations, natural treat-ments cannot substitute for synthetic drugs and surgical intervention. A person can't cure serious gunshot wounds, open fractures or a ruptured appendix with natural remedies, but many infections can be effectively controlled with the use of herbal preparations and homeopathic remedies.

There is a fine line between the legitimate boundaries of allopathic medicine and naturopathic medicine or the health field. We have seen abuses by both camps when they overstep their boundaries.

The Bach Flower preparation called "Rescue Remedy" produces amaz-ing results. It helps people gain emotional control after sustaining a serious injury. Arnica is another effective homeopathic remedy for injuries. The essential oil of Lavender can be topically used to effectively reduce the pain caused by both minor and major closed fractures.

Family Guide to Homeopathy by Dr. Andrew Lockie is a comprehensive guide. Inexpensive homeopathic kits can be purchased from Boiron or Standard Homeopathic.

Traditional Chinese medicine has made use of herbal preparations for thousands of years. One in particular, Yunnan Paiyao, was used by the Vietcong to treat gunshot wounds. The preparation is taken both topically on the wound site and orally. It is used to treat traumatic hemorrhaging, bruises and contusions and recommended for the treatment of skin infections.

Rescue Remedy is a Bach Flower remedy that relieves stress.

A similar Western remedy is the mixture of goldenseal and cayenne that can be put directly on open wounds. It facilitates clotting and suppresses infection. Goldenseal and echinacea have a natural antibiotic effect and can be taken orally for the treatment of bacterial infections. According to herbalist Dr. Christopher, cayenne, when taken orally in substantial quantities causes the vascular system to dilate, which can be helpful for chest pain caused by an obstruction to the coronary artery, i.e., heart attack.

Two excellent books about natural health care are *Prescription for Nutritional Healing* by James F. Black, M.D. and Phyllis Black, CNC, and *Anti-Aging Manual, The Encyclopedia of Natural Healing* by Joseph Marion.

Nutrition

Certain nutritional factors can protect the body from radiation damage and increase immune resistance. Most of these nutrients can be eaten ahead of time to strengthen the immune system and then taken in larger doses after radiation or disease exposure.

Vitamin E

Vitamin E is the most important free radical trap to counter the effects of radiation. Wheat germ and some unrefined vegetable oils are good sources. Oats, all leafy greens and most whole grains and nuts are reasonable sources. One of the major reasons that nitrogen or carbon dioxide is used to store foods is to displace oxygen and therefore protect vitamin E and the polyunsaturated fatty acids from oxygen damage.

Unless you spend lots of time figuring out and maximizing your intake from food sources, a daily supplement is prudent to maintain your system in the best possible condition and to build your stores for radiation protection.

The most effective form of vitamin E supplement is called alpha-to-copherol-acetate. The acetate form is synthetic but it stores much better than natural vitamin E sources. This is one case where the cheapest, drug store sale vitamins are the best buy for daily use or for long-term storage. Most people should take 200–400 IU (international unit) daily. Larger amounts (about 1,000 IU per day) are desirable after radiation exposure.

Carotenoid

Researchers are just beginning to appreciate the importance of carotenoid compounds as free radical traps. Carotenoid converts to Vitamin A which is very important to oppose infection. Green and yellow vegetables and fruits are good sources, especially pumpkins, yellow squash, sweet potatoes, yams, carrots, egg yolks and yellow fruits. Many seaweeds are excellent sources of carotenoid. A desirable level of supplementation has not been established and supplementation may not be essential if attention is paid to including sufficient highly colored yellow and green foods in the diet.

Sulfur Amino Acids

Sulfur Amino Acids, technically called methionine and cysteine, trap free radicals directly and are also essential to detoxify lipid peroxide compounds that are secondary products of radiation damage. The sulfur amino acids may be the hardest single nutrient to get enough of in our diets. Eggs are a superb source of sulfur amino acids (as well as a source of well-rounded amino acid nutrition). Most grains are rather weak in sulfur amino acid content although millet is excellent, brown rice and barley are pretty good and whole wheat is a modest but useful source.

Many types of fish are good sources of sulfur amino acids including haddock, tuna, cod and catfish. Sesame seeds and Brazil nuts are good sources. This is one of the nutrients that should be stored because treatment for radiation exposure optimally requires more than can be obtained practically from nutritional sources.

Vitamin C

Vitamin C is essential for good health and for radiation protection. It is prudent to take supplements because many other considerations come into daily meal planning and the best foods for vitamin C content are not always available (especially in a long-term food storage supply).

Increase vitamin C intake in times of severe stress, infection or injury. Vitamin C is essential in healing and wound repair.

Time-release forms are best for daily nutritional intake. The minimum daily dose is 1,000–2,000 milligrams taken at two different times.

Selenium

Selenium is a trace mineral that detoxifies peroxide products of free radicals and is an immune stimulant. Only about 100 micrograms are needed per day. It is prudent to take a 50-microgram supplement daily since it is hard to be sure how much is in the food we eat. Wheat is a major dietary source but the selenium in the wheat depends on the amount of selenium in the soil on which the wheat is grown. Other whole grains are useful sources, as are vegetables. Ocean fish and garlic are very good sources.

Selenium has been in the news for its toxicity, which is a reality at high levels. Keep dietary supplements secure and out of the reach of little children.

Polyunsaturated Fatty Acids

Common medical practice is to recommend lots of polyunsaturated fatty acids to lower blood cholesterol. Followed blindly this recommendation can present problems, because polyunsaturated fatty acids are the compounds in our bodies that are most sensitive to damage by free radicals.

Olive oil is the most healthful type of oil. It is rich in a mono-unsaturated fatty acid (called oleic acid) that is effective in lowering cholesterol but is very resistant to damage by free radicals.

Proteins

Balanced protein nutrition is required for optimum operation of almost all bodily defense mechanisms including resistance to infection, radiation and environmental toxins. These defense mechanisms require the synthesis of fresh, new protein enzymes that can only be accomplished by eating a balanced ratio of the essential amino acid building blocks within three to five hours. The key essential amino acids are lysine, isoleucine, tryptophane, and the two sulfur amino acids previously mentioned, methionine and cysteine. Obtaining this balance is the goal of combining grains with beans in the diet. Rice/soy, corn/beans, and legume soup with bread are examples of good combining.

Sanitation and Disease

Sanitation is not a luxury, it is a survival necessity. More civilians die in wars from diseases resulting from the breakdown in sanitation than from flying bullets and bombs. Modern sanitation, not immunization, is responsible for eliminating most major diseases.

Public sewer and water facilities may not function during a disaster. As a result, diseases such as cholera, typhoid and scurvy will reoccur if good sanitation practices are not maintained. Close confinement and a lack of medical care will compound the effects of poor sanitation. Following is a description of several of the major diseases that are of concern.

Typhoid Fever

Typhoid is an acute infection of the intestinal tract. The main symptom is a continual but erratic fever that can last up to four weeks. The beginning of this disease may pass unnoticed with a general malaise (bodily weakness), anorexia (lack of appetite) and headaches. During the first week, the patient's fever can rise to 104 degrees and he becomes helpless and submissive. Frequent nosebleeds are common and diarrhea and constipation are often present, accompanied by abdominal tenderness and distention. Discrete rose-colored spots may be seen on the body. The death rate is only five percent if treatment begins in the early stages.

Cholera

Cholera is an acute infection of the intestinal tract. Symptoms are a moderate diarrhea that develops into sudden violent diarrhea and vomiting. Unless the dehydration is checked, the disease can be fatal within a few days. If untreated, the death rate is 20 to 85 percent.

These two diseases, typhoid and cholera, are caused by the water, food or people being contaminated by human sewage. Common modes by which these diseases are spread between people include soiled clothing and skin and mouth contact. Once having contracted either typhoid or cholera, the person can be a carrier for days or weeks, spreading it to others through skin contact.

Hantavirus

Every so often there is another article in the newspapers about someone contracting Hantavirus or mice being found which are infected with the virus. Hantavirus is transmitted to people through airborne particles of mouse droppings and nesting materials. The virus grows in cells lining the lungs and when the immune system attacks the infection, small holes develop. As a result, liquid fills the lungs and death occurs. It takes about two weeks for an infected person to get sick. Symptoms are similar to flu. Two to three days after initial symptoms the body collapses and 24 to 48 hours later, death occurs.

Keep your food storage areas liberally distributed with bar bait or De-Con type mouse poison. Dark, uninhabited areas with improperly packaged food will result in eventual mouse infestations.

If you end up with an infestation, do not sweep up or vacuum droppings and nesting material until disinfecting with 10 parts water to one part household bleach. Spray the area and let it soak for 15 minutes. Carpets can be cleaned with a steam cleaner.

Hepatitis

Hepatitis is usually very slow to get started and begins with anorexia, vague abdominal discomfort and nausea. Fatality ranges from one to twenty percent even when treated. Hepatitis A is transmitted by personal contact and from handling contaminated water or food. Food is a more common mode of transfer than water. If food is washed off with contaminated water, it becomes infected. This disease is commonly transferred by food handlers with the disease in the incubation period when the symptoms are not noticeable. The prevention of this disease is maintaining cleanliness—washing hands after using the toilet, washing before preparing food, keeping soiled clothing away from food, and washing soiled clothing with plenty of soap and water.

In addition to a strict adherence to all cleanliness procedures, wash dishes, cups and silverware in a rinse containing one tablespoon of Clorox-type bleach to a quart of water.

Sanitation Practices

Good sanitation practices can make the difference between health and illness.

Most of us do not have to do much these days to dispose of human wastes. Modern plumbing and flush toilets have enabled us to distance ourselves from this sometimes-unpleasant task. But those who live in rural areas know that if you have a well pump, any loss of power disables your normal means of flushing the toilet. If you have surface water nearby—a swimming pool, pond, stream or swamp—you can fill a bucket and use it to flush the toilet by pouring it into the toilet bowel. If you live in the city this method works only if the municipal sewer system is still operating its pumps so the sewage has some place to go.

If these options fail then you will have to resort to a more primitive approach. Camping supply stores sell stool-type toilets that come with either a bucket or a plastic bag arrangement. With either option there is usually a disposable bag liner and deodorizer. When the bag liner gets full you take it out, put a twist tie on the bag and get rid of it.

The next question is "Where do I get rid of it?" If you don't have power, water or sewer, chances are you won't have trash removal either. Dig a hole in your back yard and bury the bags. Do not bury waste products within 50 feet of a water source.

If you do not have one of these wonder buckets, use your shovel. Dig a trench or hole two to three feet deep in the back yard. Take the seat off

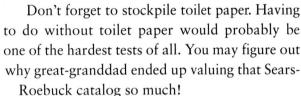

your toilet and rig some sort of support frame over the hole to put the seat on. If you have wood ashes from a fireplace or wood stove, save these and put them in a bucket next to this privy with an empty tin can. Every time you use the hole, sprinkle some ashes in the hole afterwards. It will keep down the smell and flies. Or throw some loose dirt on top. Exposed feces attracts flies which can spread disease!

Don't forget to stockpile toilet paper. Having to do without toilet paper would probably be one of the hardest tests of all. You may figure out why great-granddad ended up valuing that Sears-Roebuck catalog so much!

Afterwards, wash your hands in a water-bleach solution. Have a stockpile of bleach and soap.

Bleach, soap and toilet paper become high value barter items in hard times.

For other types of trash, a good metal burn barrel works wonders.

A camping toilet is a useful tool when the city sewer system stops working.

CHAPTER 14
Security

Security concerns bring up very sensitive issues. The trend today is toward disarming the public. Anything relating to gun ownership, personal defense or property protection is considered politically incorrect. If the local media picks up on any such activity, they may accuse you of intending some sort of confrontation with the government.

However, the security of your person and property are legitimate concerns in this day and age. Security activities are not based on an intent to conflict with the government, but a concern that during a national crisis there won't be enough government to ensure law and order.

In the case of major regional disturbances, riots and disorders, the first priority of any individual, civilian or policeman will be to protect their own property and family. Law enforcement personnel may not be on the job helping to maintain order if their families and property are in jeopardy.

If a life-threatening incident occurs, try to contact the local authorities by radio and ask them how they would like you to deal with the situation. Document and record if possible any such urgent communications. A major disaster is not necessarily going to bring the end of the world and you might have to answer for rash actions after the dust settles.

Non-lethal Deterrents

Be creative. Have non-lethal alternatives to violence that you can try first. Pepper spray is a good choice and is readily available from your local camping supply store. Hikers and hunters carry it in the backcountry to protect themselves from bear attacks. Mace is another option, but pepper spray is the more popular self-defense spray.

Firearms

If you decide to pursue gun ownership, consider taking a class in basic gun use. These courses are available in most areas. There are some fairly good prerequisite courses for concealed weapon permits. These provide a basic understanding of legal issues, gun safety, shooting and loading proficiency and greater confidence. Firearms may give you the ability to take control of a threatening situation. In a crisis they enable you to make a show of force, which can prevent crime and violence. History has clearly shown that deterrence is a key to the maintenance of peace.

CHAPTER 15
The Psychology of Survival

Most survival manuals emphasize the physical aspects of a survival situation, but the most critical factor may well be the person's attitude and his will to live. In a crisis situation it is important to focus on "How can I improve this position?" as opposed to "What a horrible position I am in." The primary mental assets for the survivor are belief in oneself and a positive attitude.

The primary underlying psychological fear in any survival situation is the fear of lack of control.

As a result many people in survival situations suffer extreme stress. Stress is not a direct function of events, but it is caused by the perception or view one takes of events. Perception in many cases is nothing more than an imagined and unreal overlay. Just the perception of loss of control results in stress. Studies have shown that when different individuals are exposed to the same challenging external factors, those who believe they have no control over the outcome suffer more stress than those who believe they have some element of control.

Taking immediate and constructive action during a crisis helps to re-establish a sense of control. By doing something, even if it is just a small first step, the individual can start to regain control of a situation and not just become helpless victims of circumstance.

What is the best way to handle survival stress? How can you become one of the small percentage of people who react to an accident or survival situation with maximum effectiveness? The following are a series of coping mechanisms that can maintain effective self-control in a crisis situation.

Decision and Action

Once a decision has been made as to the best course of immediate action, doubt and uncertainty are removed. The movement to action helps bring a feeling of regaining control over the situation. Inactivity in a high state of arousal is very stressful. Action helps to use up energy from a body in a high state of arousal and decreases the stress. If the action improves the situation, even if only in a marginal way, this is even more beneficial.

Goals and Management

Do not try to solve a major survival situation all at once. Determine what are the most immediate needs and deal with them in manageable units on a one-at-a-time basis. This action can greatly reduce the tendency to become overwhelmed and paralyzed in the face of disaster.

Focus on the Immediate

Define the tasks necessary to meet immediate needs, then focus on completing each task. Controlling the mind's focus is the key to success. Most people allow their attention to passively follow the random wanderings of the mind. The rambling nature of the mind keeps a person's focus predominantly in the past or in the future, with very little time actually spent concentrating on the present.

Keep attention focused in the present for the best possible outcome. There is no benefit in wasting energy on regretting mistakes made or worrying about future events. Fear, stress and urgency are byproducts of focusing on imagined negative outcomes in the future. The future is nothing more than speculation. When the crisis has passed, then review events and learn from mistakes.

Eliminate emotional turmoil by disciplining attention to focus on the present and by accepting whatever is happening without jumping to negative conclusions. Fortunately, during a crisis the urgency of the situation helps to disarm the mind's overpowering tendency to wander. Thus many individuals are able to exert greater control over mental functions.

Like any ability, focusing in the present is a direct product of the strength one develops over time through exercise and patterning. If you intend to be in control of yourself during a crisis, start now to discipline and get control of your wandering mental functions.

"I'm learning in my old age that the only thing you can do to keep your sanity is to stay in the moment."

—William Dafoe

Ritual and Order

The amount of stress experienced is in direct relationship to the degree of change and the degree of perceived loss of control over events. The sooner one can bring order into a survival situation through the establishing of rituals, such as eating, building a fire, and signaling for help, the sooner stress will be reduced.

Switching Off

The immediate situation is shut out and one focuses the mind on more pleasurable experiences or imagines a time beyond the disaster when everyone is at last recovered and safe. This can either be selective or total. Selective switching off can be seen in the repression of emotions when dealing with extremely traumatic accidents that require quick and effective aid to be administered. Total switching off can only be achieved when it is safe to do so, for instance, when one is safely in a survival shelter or when just sitting out a storm.

Humor

Humor is a very effective tool for decreasing stress by being able to see another side of what may be a serious situation. Humor can provide emotional release in a positive and restorative manner after a positive action has taken place.

All of these coping mechanisms can be used successfully in a variety of situations—from a traumatic accident, to an outdoor survival situation, to widespread disaster. Individually, these tactics can also be used on a regular basis to reduce the stress we all encounter in our daily lives. The more familiar they become, the more prepared we will be to use them in a major crisis.

Psychological Responses to Disaster

It is important to understand some of the ways people react during emergencies, disasters, and unusually adverse conditions. It is difficult to predetermine exactly what individual reactions will be. There are, however, fairly common reactions that can be predicted. Understanding these reactions will help the individual and the group to maintain some sort of objectivity, and to implement remedies and prevention.

The natural psychological and emotional reactions which people have as a result of a disaster include fear, terror, panic, emotional containment, and depression.

Fear

Fear is a normal reaction. Within certain limits, fear fulfills a function. Fear serves as a warning and an aid. Fear mobilizes the body's reserved strength and increases its physical abilities. Fear allows people to accomplish feats which otherwise would be unthinkable. Fear can be a useful driving force.

The symptoms that people show when under the effects of fear are an increased need for contact (conversation provides a sense of security) and increased inner tension, which can result in the involuntary shaking of the hands, sweating, flushing, palpitations of the heart, and pressure on the bladder. Fear is usually short term and does not have long-term adverse side effects.

Terror

Terror is fear that has intensified and is usually provoked by an unexpected danger. Suddenness and surprise are essential ingredients for producing a terror reaction. Terror is a storm of emotion that expresses itself violently and irrationally and can increase the danger in a situation. Terror is an emotional obliteration of the will, reason, and common sense. The mind is completely flooded and it is unable to clearly evaluate the real level of danger. The power to deliberate is put to flight by the absolute emotion of terror. Terror overwhelms the ego and paralyzes certain mental facilities.

Terror manifests in two phases. The first reaction is apathy. This will be seen as an absolute inhibition and immobility; in other words, terror-stricken. Typically, terrorized people in dangerous situations can become indifferent to their own safety and the destruction going on around them. The second phase of terror that follows apathy is the impulse to flee. This is usually indiscriminate, without common sense. Both phases can involve a dazed condition and a loss of memory.

Terror is an emotional reaction that generally does not benefit the individual, but increases vulnerability to injury and disaster.

There's a further danger: terror may become explosively contagious.

One significant indication of when normal fear is on the verge of dissolving into terror is when the need to talk increases and people begin to scream. The raising of the level of the voice indicates an acceleration of emotions that are beginning to overwhelm the individual's faculties of logic and control. When people are showing signs of trembling, walking back and forth and doing unnecessary things, this indicates a buildup of inner tension. The only thing to do for a person suffering from terror is to isolate them. If such an individual is violent, they need to be brought under control for their own good and to prevent infecting others. Methods of force should be limited to keeping them quiet with a gag and tying them up. If the means is available, sedate the individual.

Panic

Panic is a group emotion. Panic, like terror, is explosively contagious and spreads quickly. Panic is a reaction to a suggestion of danger that may or may not be real. When an individual loses his power to exercise common sense, he can easily be swept away by group emotions. Panic is a mass psychosis that can drive a whole group to irrational acts.

Panic is grounded in the herd instinct and need for security. People fulfill their needs for security through group contact and interaction. It's seen in day-to-day life when people find places in social groups. People feel protected by the similar behavior of those around them. This is seen at sporting events when an individual in the group lets the imitation instinct take over and thus fulfills a need for community feeling.

Panic usually starts with one weak-willed person and spreads lightning-fast throughout the group by way of suggestion. Those who usually have the ability to control their inner anxiety can also be swept along with this herd reaction of abandoning one's ego and dissolving into the group. Strength of character and a well-exercised willpower are the only deterrents to being swept away in such group reactions.

Emotional Containment

Emotional containment is a positive, involuntary reaction that some people experience in the face of a dire emergency. The dominating emotional impact of the incident is totally suppressed. This allows for a better possibility of control and common sense. Under emotional containment one can think clearly and act purposefully. An extremely focused consciousness accompanies emotional containment, which shuts out anything going on outside the person's immediate surroundings.

Depression

Many factors can cause depression, including disaster or personal loss. Faced with the unknown, concerns for the fate of close friends and relatives, a perceived inability to improve one's situation, or feeling out of control of one's future, a situation could easily become overwhelming. This could result in a breakdown of normal psychological defenses, and thus a downward spiral of mental and emotional despair, ultimately resulting in emotional depression.

Dysphoric mood is a common symptom associated with depressed individuals. This includes an all-pervasive sense of doom and gloom. As this symptom progresses, individuals lose interest in things that were previously important to them or gave them enjoyment or gratification.

Treating Depression

Early recognition and treatment is vital.

It is important how you make contact with a person suffering from depression. Don't attempt to approach him in an aggressive or demanding manner, such as telling him to "snap out of it." Try to make a gentle, understanding contact, with the objective of securing rapport. On the other hand, don't indulge in pity. Get him to tell you what happened or what is going on.

Vigorous exercise increases the production of the neurotransmitters norepinephrine and serotonin in the brain. These naturally occurring chemicals act as natural antidepressants and tend to elevate moods.

Do not give a depressed individual alcohol or other depressants, such as tranquilizers, antihistamines, codeine cough suppressants or any other similar-acting medications.

When people are kept busy in the aftermath of a disaster they don't have excess time to dwell on their problems. Make or create work if necessary to keep everyone occupied.

During one of the major World War II Pacific sea battles, a U.S. aircraft carrier was badly damaged, almost sunk, and took massive casualties. The captain opted not to abandon the burning, listing ship and managed to stabilize the vessel. En route back to San Francisco, he kept the surviving crew working around the clock repairing what damage they could, cleaning up the devastation, recovering bodies and body parts and giving them sea burials. The captain did this intentionally so that the remaining crew, who had lived through a nightmare, would not have time to dwell on the tragedy and carnage they had experienced.

Predictable Psychological Reactions to Disaster

A disaster can be segmented into seven phases, each associated with predictable psychological reactions.

Warning Phase

During the warning phase people experience anxiety and denial.

Alarm Phase

During the alarm phase psychological reactions include increased activity and panic.

Impact Phase

During the impact phase people tend to become emotionally stunned, overwhelmed and shocked. This is typified by aimless wandering.

Inventory Phase

During the inventory phase those stunned by the impact of the disaster are confused and disoriented as they start to regain their senses. People take inventory of their situation by beginning to assess their losses and the current level of danger in an attempt to figure out how to cope with the situation. Once people feel assured that things are reasonably under control and that they are safe again, some of these people are able to start helping and assisting other victims of the disaster. Research indicates that about half the people in disasters will move quickly through the warning, alarm and impact phases into an adaptive mode and thus be able to help other victims. The other half will stay stunned and thus remain in a victim mode.

Once the inventory phase starts the first thing to do is to enlist and organize those who have made it through the warning, alarm and impact phases, and start assisting less fortunate victims.

The second step is to set up a triage program, sorting victims according to a hierarchy of need (who needs the most service right now, who needs the least) in order to utilize limited resources for those who have the most need.

This is a practicality and a reality that rescuers and medical-aid personnel have to face in a disaster. Resources should be concentrated on those with serious but salvageable injuries. This involves making hard decisions. In a typical major disaster there aren't enough immediate medical services available to treat all the injured at once.

Rescue Phase

During the rescue phase victims are happy to be alive and euphoric; but this reaction is short-lived. Very quickly reality sets in and the victims begin to realize the seriousness of the situation. Thus, euphoria will often turn to anger, depression, or desolation.

Recovery Phase

During the recovery phase victims start experiencing a sense of relief. The immediate danger seems to be over, but bouts of anxiety and fearfulness tend to reoccur. This insecurity and anxiety is not over concerns for here-and-now situations, as is the case in the rescue phase, but is caused by concerns about the future.

Thinking and focusing on the future is a key indicator of the recovery phase. Even though victims are having a negative response to the future, they are moving through it. This is a positive psychological sign.

Reconstruction Phase

During the reconstruction phase, victims have adapted to change and they have essentially returned to a functional level. They are now at a level where they can mobilize their internal resources, assess external resources, and begin to function in a helper/responder role. All the human faculties essentially return to a minimally productive level. However, the one thing that needs to be watched for in this last phase is the potential for relapse.

Some will assume that they have dealt with the disaster and put it behind them, but they don't realize that resolution and recovery is an ongoing process. This involves dealing with reemerging feelings, reverting and repeating some of the phases. Thus, some people may relapse into a deeper state of any one of these phases.

Disaster Myths

There are a number of commonly accepted myths regarding people's reactions to disasters. Examining these myths will help us better understand, prepare for and cope with disasters.

Myth: People heed warnings.

The first myth is that people will heed warnings. People generally do not heed warnings. Historical research on the Pompeii disaster indicates that there were many warnings from nature and people. But while people generally ignore warnings, they will listen if the alarm is repeated by trusted leaders, neighbors, friends, and family.

Myth: People always panic in a crisis.

In fact, mass panic occurs in only 10 percent of disasters, and then only when there is no clear evidence of an escape route or protection. The existence of some level of preparedness becomes a key element in helping people psychologically deal with the crisis when it arrives.

Myth: Disaster means society will remain psychologically devastated.

It's not true that in a disaster, the entire social structure of the community will remain psychologically devastated.

People have a miraculous resiliency. History has shown that people do have the ability to rise to the occasion and deal with what needs to be dealt with. This is not to say that it does not happen without pain, mistakes or difficulty. The truth is that communities restore themselves to normal functioning, and only about half the people will need help coping with depression or anxiety.

Disasters have often brought people of various religions, races, ethnic groups and socioeconomic levels together. Many experience deep bonding with individuals that they wouldn't have even talked to before. This happens because in times of crisis, people naturally tend to go to their hearts and pull together as a group.

Factors that Affect Human Reaction to Disaster

Many factors affect people's reactions to disaster. These include factors which tend to escalate negative reactions as well as factors that can have a mitigating effect.

Escalating Factors

There are certain factors that can escalate the individual's negative reaction to a disaster. These factors include:

1. Severity of injury

2. The intensity of the incident

3. The length of time that the crisis lasts

4. The occurrence of more than one disastrous event in the same time frame.

This duration factor can be very difficult to deal with when people don't know how long the disaster is going to continue. The simultaneous occurrence of multiple disastrous events compounds the intensity of the overall disaster.

Mitigating Factors

There are variables that can reduce negative reactions to disaster. These include:

1. A quick, well-organized rescue effort.

    The speed, comprehensiveness and organization of the disaster relief and rescue effort obviously mitigate the negative impact of a disaster.

2. The existence of a family or community network.

    It is important to recognize who is a stranger and who isn't in the disaster situation. Try to get people matched up with people they know. If they don't know anybody, get them introduced and start that networking happening.

Variable Factors

Age

The young and the elderly are the most vulnerable in a disaster. They are the most concerned about security. They feel the least capable of coping because their resources are usually more limited. Their physical capabilities are more limited and, particularly with children, they haven't developed the capacity to really understand what is going on. The very elderly may have gone back to the childlike state because of dementia where they don't fully understand what is going on.

Objectives for Managing the Disaster and the Victims

Basic objectives for disaster management personnel include:

1. Safety first!

2. Bring the disaster situation under control. Prevent more people from getting hurt or killed.

3. Organize and provide basic services for displaced persons, including food, clothing, shelter, and security.

4. Assist displaced victims in finding relatives or friends who can better help them through the crisis. If relatives or friends are not available, match them up with someone they know. If no familiar persons are available, then pair the displaced victim up with someone who is outgoing. A person or family willing to make them part of their family group is ideal.

5. Encourage victims to return to "normal" schedules. In a disaster situation there will be no real normal schedule, but try to approximate one. Try to get people on a regular eating and sleeping schedule. Get people working on activities that utilize their skills as soon as they can be moved through their own traumatic response.

Protect victims as much as possible from further stress. Provide psychological counseling services. If trained personnel are not available then find someone who seems to have a natural listening ear for people to vent their problems, emotions, and anxieties. Counselors should avoid making statements such as "Well, it could have been worse," or "You're lucky to be alive."

Counselors should be very perceptive. This means not only listening to the words, but also listening to what the underlying message is, and what the behavior is saying. If there is an incompatibility, the behavior usually provides a truer message than the words. A gentle physical touch and a calm soothing voice will go a long way in helping victims recover from the trauma of a disaster.

What has been learned about disasters is that people should contain their feelings. It is not the time to help people cry and express their feelings. It's not a problem if someone cries or wails, if that is what is going on with them. However, they should get to a point where they feel more emotional control. They have enough lack of control going on in their lives without feeling emotionally out of control. There will be plenty of time later to set up some groups to help people work through their feelings, to purge the negative emotions.

Containment is a good by-word all the way through. Contain. Protect. Organize. Bring things back into focus to help people move into the coping phase. Encourage the defense mechanisms. Don't encourage a lack of reality about what's happening, but do encourage people to feel that, internally and externally, they can feel safe.

Reassure people that what they are experiencing is normal. Whatever they are experiencing, there is no such thing as abnormal in a crisis or disaster situation. Reassure them that there is nothing wrong with experiencing what they are experiencing. Reassure people that they have it within themselves to survive.

Critical Incident Stress

The September 11 New York World Trade Center disaster was one of the most significant single events in U.S. history in terms of inflicted emotional trauma. The unique and tragic aspect of this particular disaster was the loss of 300 rescuers and emergency responders.

"Nothing could have completely prepared us for what befell New York on September 11," said New York City Department of Mental Health Commissioner Neal Cohen, M.D. "Some police and fire companies sustained overwhelming personnel losses. Those who survived have, and can be expected to have, unique adjustment problems."

Critical incident stress is the normal reaction of normal individuals to abnormal events. Some of the conditions that cause critical incident stress are events, emergencies or disasters that result in sudden or unexpected death. These can burden rescue personnel, family, and bystanders with stress.

This stress is often magnified if the victim was a child, if the emergency involved carnage or great human suffering, if a death occurred after a prolonged rescue attempt, or if a victim at the incident was expressing uncontrolled emotion. The emotions caused by these types of events can surface again and again long after the event is over, causing those involved to feel like they are on an emotional roller coaster. This is a normal response to an abnormal event.

The individual's reaction to stress can be either acute or delayed. The acute stress response (immediate reaction) to the incident can include becoming physically ill, the inability to function, becoming immobilized, and mental or emotional breakdown.

The delayed stress reaction that results in behavioral problems is referred to as post-traumatic stress disorder (PTSD). PTSD is a serious problem with fire, EMS (Emergency Medical Services), and law enforcement personnel nationwide. It is the major cause for people leaving the EMS field today.

If this stress is ignored or suppressed, it can lead to physical and emotional symptoms as well as behavioral problems that incapacitate valuable people.

Common Stress Reaction Symptoms

Some people, particularly those who avoid dealing with their emotional reactions, may find themselves increasingly reliving their trauma. The following are twenty signals that indicate "I'm stuck."

- Intrusive images—distressing memories, thoughts, nightmares, flashbacks

- Distress at exposure to events that resemble or symbolize the event

- Avoids thoughts and emotions connected with the incident, or activities that arouse memories of the trauma

- Numbing or restricted range of emotional responsiveness

- Excessive stress reactions

- Hyper-vigilance

- Overreaction/under-reaction/risk taking

- Increased irritability, anger, or rage

- Obsession with the incident

- Current incident can trigger feelings associated with past events; emotional impact of old and new situations becomes overwhelming

- Self-doubt, guilt, second guessing of oneself, feelings of inadequacy, obsession with perceived mistakes

- A growing sense of isolation: "No one understands what I'm feeling."

- Intense or sustained feelings of depression, grief, loss of control

- Mental confusion: increased distractibility, difficulty concentrating or making decisions, poor judgment

- Development of suspiciousness in dealing with others

- Relationship problems: peer/supervisory/family; withdrawal from others

- Decline in work performance

- Having little or no noticeable initial reaction to the incident, but reactions are triggered months later

- Self-destructive behavior: substance abuse, poor judgment

In rare cases, suicidal thinking may result from feelings of depression, guilt, despair, and anger at oneself.

Ways to Reduce Reactions to Stress

Prior to an Incident:

Pre-incident training

Prepare with reading, discussion, and training. Get information before an event as to what you might expect in the different possible scenarios.

Teamwork

Spend time with the people who are in your disaster response group ahead of time to develop a good working relationship.

Communication skills

Learn communication skills. Marshall Rosenberg's Non-violent Communication techniques provide simple yet profound tools. Parent-training books give instruction on how to talk with children and teenagers.

During or After an Incident:

Be physically active

Within the first 24 to 48 hours, alternate periods of strenuous physical exercise with relaxation. Take breaks. Don't get into the self-defeating situation of "they can't do without me" because if you don't take any breaks, they'll have to do without you. You will collapse at some point. So take a break before this happens.

Structure your time; keep busy

Accept yourself

Understand that your reactions are normal; don't label yourself as crazy. Give yourself permission to feel rotten.

Talk to people

Talk is the most healing medicine. Reach out; people do care. Spend time with others.

Keep your life as normal as possible; don't make any big life changes.

Eat well

Supplement your diet with Vitamin C, B Stress vitamins, calcium and magnesium.

Get some sleep

Power naps are 15 minutes of sleep to get the energy back. Regenerating sleep requires between $1^1/2$ to 3 hours to move through the REM sleep cycle.

Maintain a sense of hope

Remember that your survival effort is important. It is important in terms of the survival of your family and loved ones. Remind yourself and remind one another why you are doing this. It may seem so chaotic at first that you'll wonder, "Why are we doing this?" Some may even wonder, "Wouldn't it have been better for us to have just stood under the bomb and let it drop on us?" You may imagine that no one will think this, but your group will have the same problems as any other group in the world that has gone through traumatic experiences.

Critical Incident Stress Debriefing

Maintain emotional control in the interest of stability, but express pent-up emotion as soon as it is appropriate. This is referred to as critical incident stress debriefing. Psychologists have developed a model that helps first responders get through the emotional stress that comes with their job. If you feel that you, or someone you know, may be suffering from post-traumatic stress disorder, seek out help from the psychological professionals in your community.

Psychologically Preparing Oneself for Disaster

People can condition and prepare themselves psychologically for dealing with difficult and stressful situations. It is possible to consciously develop a calm and composed attitude in an emergency medical response situation. Having an emotional reaction to an emergency, i.e., being flustered, in a hurry, and being excited causes you to fumble, make mistakes and not follow established procedures. Such a reaction in no way helps the situation or the people involved. It is better to consciously be in control of your emotions, slow down and take your time doing things effectively the first time.

One can condition oneself to be in emotional control under other contemplated emergency situations. This potentially includes not being overwhelmed by carnage, dead bodies and people who are seriously maimed. If you allow yourself to be swept away by flood tides of emotion, you will not be able to help those around you who are in distress and seriously need assistance.

In his book *Awaken the Giant Within,* Anthony Robbins discusses "The Law of Reinforcement:" any pattern of behavior that is continually reinforced will become an automatic and conditioned response. Anything we fail to reinforce will eventually dissipate.

Localized vs. Cataclysmic Disaster

Disasters can be categorized as local or cataclysmic. The first and most common category includes localized disasters, such as floods, fires, earthquakes, hurricanes or large accidents where the emergency services in the area are strained or incapacitated, but help from the unaffected surrounding areas is able to respond and stabilize the situation. The second category describes a catastrophic or cataclysmic disaster that impacts a wide geographic area. This is so massive that little or no relief aid or help can be expected from any outside source.

What this means is that those involved will have to wear two different hats: that of the victim, and that of the rescuer. This seriously complicates the recovery and rescue process. During common disasters, like the earthquake in Northridge, California, most of the rescue and relief help came from outside the Northridge area. These rescuers did not have to worry about the fate of family members, friends and relatives, their houses or their belongings, and thus they were able to concentrate their entire attention on helping victims.

During a cataclysmic disaster, the rescuers are going to be in the position of having been affected by the disaster as well as having to help others. Preparedness and rehearsal can significantly improve one's ability to function and cope with such a dual role disaster situation. The more prepared a person is and the more they have thought through a potential disaster scenario, the more likely they will be in that 50 percent group which moves quickly through the traumatic response to the disaster, and thereby is able to move into helping other victims.

Dealing with Children's Reactions

Preparation will help parents deal with children's fears and anxieties. During a disaster the primary concern of any parent is the physical safety of their children and the family as a whole. But as a result, the disaster's emotional impact on the child is frequently neglected.

The average child's environment consists of certain regularities: the presence of parents, awakening in the morning, preparing for school, meeting with the same teacher and the same children, playing with friends and sleeping in their own bed. Establishing a familiar routine as soon as possible is very helpful.

The child expects dependability from adults and certainly from the forces of nature. For the preschooler, life is filled with daily routines. When there is an interruption in this natural flow of life, the child experiences anxiety and fear. How the adults help the child to resolve these "problem times" may have a lasting effect on the child.

Fear is a normal reaction to any danger that threatens life or well-being. The child is afraid of injury or death. He is afraid that the disaster might reoccur. He is also afraid of being separated from his family and being left alone.

The child, who is dependent on adults for love, care, security and food, fears most the loss of his parents and being left alone. Even a usually courageous child may react with fear to an event that threatens the family. Since most adults also respond to disaster with normal and natural fear, the child becomes terrified, taking parental fears as proof that the danger is real.

So it is very important for the family to remain together. This provides immediate reassurance to a child. Children should not be left alone at a shelter while the parents go out for supplies or possessions or to inspect possible damage. If the child is left alone, his fears will increase and subsequently so will his clinging behavior.

Although parents experience fear, they have the maturity to cope. A demonstration of strength will reassure the child. However, it will not harm the child to let him know that you are also afraid. As a matter of fact, it is good to put these feelings into words. This sharing will encourage him to talk about his own feelings or fears. Then the parents will have an opportunity to explore these fears and reassure the child.

Explain what is happening and what to expect in the near future. A child may express his fears in play or in actions. If these fears are unrealistic, explain and reassure him. You may have to repeat yourself many times. Don't stop explaining just because you have told him this once before.

Fear can be viewed as that part of your mind that looks into the future, imagines a negative outcome and accepts it as real. Controlling your mind and insisting that it imagine a positive outcome, success rather than failure, can be a very powerful tool. From athletes about to enter into a competition to parents waiting for the completion of their child's surgery to a group of people looking toward the outcome of a natural disaster, fear can be greatly diminished by becoming mentally tough. Explain this technique to your children and practice it yourself.

The most frequently reported problem with children occurs at bedtime. The child may have difficulty falling asleep. He may wake up often during the night or he may have nightmares. It is necessary to be somewhat flexible regarding bedtime in a survival situation. Bedtime may be delayed when the child is anxious and wants to talk longer, but a limit should be set. It is natural for a child to want to be close to his parents and for the parents to want to have their children near to them.

A child can and should be included in recovery activities. Involvement reassures a child. For the parents of a very young child, the task is more difficult. Such a child may need more physical care and more holding. This makes it harder for parents to attend to the other things that should be done. Unfortunately, there is no shortcut. If the child's needs are not met, there will be continuing problems, even after the disaster.

The content of this section on children and disasters was drawn from a pamphlet titled "Coping with Children's Reactions to Disasters," written by the San Fernando Valley Child Guidance Clinic.

Death and Dying

Death is not a popular subject but it needs to be covered. All of us could be faced with an inordinate exposure to death at any time. A friend of mine experienced a near-death situation when he was 19 years old. He said that the one thing he recalled distinctly from the experience was the thought that no one had, in any way, prepared him for this.

Death is the ultimate threat. Many people today view death as the opposite of life, the complete end of everything. The idea of the extinction of self can be a terrifying concept.

Death is a taboo subject, too terrible to think about. Consequently, many people have not developed a realistic concept of death or a means of dealing with it. This is especially true in the case of those who are young and full of life. The general social practice for dealing with death is to avoid talking about it and to spend as little time as possible with dying people.

In less developed third-world countries and agrarian cultures, people are better equipped to deal with death. In rural environments, children grow up with a closer relationship to nature; they are exposed to the cycles of life and death in the changing of the seasons and in the shorter life spans of pets and livestock. Modern urban living separates people from the cycles of nature and fosters false attitudes of immunity from the effects of nature and the inevitability of death. The advance of modern medicine and the subsequent increase in the average life span have also contributed to an illusion that man has mastered death.

Fifty years ago, a major portion of American culture was centered around a more rural, agrarian structure which included a close-knit family life. This family structure usually included a large circle of aunts, uncles, cousins and grandparents living in the same house or in close proximity. If a parent died, other family members were readily available to assume the position of the deceased parent.

Today's modern family unit is usually limited to a father, mother, and children. As a result, family members tend to have stronger emotional investments in each other. In the event of the death of a family member, the sense of loss seems to be far greater and there is not necessarily someone readily available to fill the void.

Grief and Loss

The unexpected death of a close friend or loved one can cause a person to feel lost and uneasy with intangible and frightening thoughts. Grief invariably follows death. Grief is an emotional reaction that occurs when a tie of love is severed or we experience a significant loss.

Loss is an inevitable part of growth and everyday life. The experience of loss begins with birth and the separation from the warm, safe environment of the womb. Throughout a child's early development, he discovers new objects in his environment, develops attachments to some, and subsequently experiences loss when these objects are removed. Examples of this phenomenon might include weaning from the breast or bottle and the separation from a stuffed toy. Homesickness is a mild grief reaction to a separation from or loss of familiar surroundings.

Learning and maturing involves adaptive responses and effective mechanisms for coping with loss. But when a loss is traumatic, normal coping mechanisms may not be sufficient.

The Grieving/Healing Process

Grief is the emotional suffering that results from loss. The grieving process has been compared with the healing of a tissue wound. Successful grieving, like successful tissue healing, follows a predictable sequence. Like healing from a tissue wound, emotional healing takes time.

The grief process has a generally predictable course with fairly consistent symptoms, but the way each individual experiences grief will vary depending on their age, sex, ethnic background, past experience with death and individual coping patterns.

Severe grief causes a breakdown in normal coping patterns, yet some semblance of habitual response is usually retained. For example, the person who meets all of his life crises with denial will inevitably use denial when faced with sudden loss. Those who are openly emotional in every phase of their lives will be highly emotional in grieving.

Some responses to loss and grief may not conform to stereotypes and standards of conduct which most of us have inadvertently acquired during our lives. For example, persons who do not cry as the result of the death of a loved one are sometimes perceived as not being affected by the loss. The person who jokes even when faced with severe loss is felt to be behaving inappropriately and others around this individual may disapprove. In reality, no judgments should be made in this type of situation. People will cope with death in the best way they can and the individual's surface appearance does not necessarily reflect the depth of their emotional grief. Understand and support them whatever their process.

Shock and Denial

The first reaction to news of a death is usually shock and denial. This is often followed by a numb or dazed state whereby the person attempts to shut out conscious acknowledgment that the death occurred. The affected person may start carrying out automatic activities as though nothing happened. Another reaction is for the person to sit motionless, in deep introversion, making it difficult for anyone to communicate with them.

After the initial shock response, some people carry on as if nothing had happened. These people immediately begin to take care of the necessary arrangements, comfort and support other members of the family, and seem to accept the death as a reality. It is important to realize that while this person may have accepted the loss intellectually, they have suppressed the emotional impact of the death and are still in a state of partial denial. Very often this state persists through the funeral preparations and burial. These people are described as "taking it well" or "holding up well."

Perhaps what is really going on is that the grieving person is attempting to protect himself from overwhelming grief through denial. Shock and denial are more intense when the death is sudden and unexpected. The grief-stricken survivor may move into shock and denial within a matter of minutes of learning of a death or it may take weeks.

Crying

Crying is a typical response in this stage and should be encouraged. Crying is a legitimate release in the presence of death for both males and females. When men lose their customary control of emotions, they need reassurance and support because they feel ashamed of their inability to regain their composure.

Anger

Anger may be displayed in the second stage of the grieving process. This anger may be irrationally directed at anyone who the grieving person imagines must have allowed or contributed to his loved one's death. This anger is more a manifestation of a person's feelings of frustration and helplessness and their inability to do anything about it. Anger may also be felt toward another family member who somehow failed in an obligation toward the deceased. Anger may end up self-directed if the person feels himself to be somehow at fault.

People around a grieving person often are more tolerant of crying than anger. Do not take it personally or be offended. Remain calm and compassionate until the anger subsides.

Occasionally, a grieving person will have the fear that they are going insane. Those who express this fear need to be quickly reassured that the feelings they are having are a natural part of the grieving process and the feelings will eventually go away.

Guilt

Parents tend to feel guilt over the death of a child and may berate themselves or each other. Parents may even injure themselves in an impulsive gesture of aggression or self-destruction. All bereaved persons probably feel guilt to some degree as they search their minds for ways in which they may have failed the loved one. Persons mourning a loss should be allowed to express their feelings of guilt. These expressions frequently begin with the phrase, "If only I had done this (or had not done that)...." Such expressions are a normal component of the grief response and need to be expressed.

It is important to let the person express his guilt feelings freely. Listen empathetically and after he has had a chance to express his feelings then offer reassurance that will help to relieve the guilt. One possible response would be, "I think I understand how you feel. It's natural for you to feel this way right now, but you may feel differently about it later."

Mourning

Mourning is the third stage in the grieving. During this final stage, which may go on for a year or more, the bereaved person works through feelings of loss and resumes a normal life.

When someone is in shock, their body protects them from the pain of grief. Later—days, weeks, or months—they feel the pain more intensely. When this starts to happen so much later than expected it can feel like a downhill slide. In fact, the body is sensing that they are ready to begin the process of grieving and allows the shock to wear off. As much as it would be nice to avoid these painful feelings, the way out is the way through.

Supporting People in the Event of a Death

When trying to comfort a person who has just suffered the loss of a loved one, do not say "I know how you feel." The reality is that people who are not suffering from the loss have no idea what the grieving individual is going through. Such a well-intended yet unhelpful remark can elicit an outrageous response. The best thing you can do is be there. Offer support. Take care of details for the affected individuals. Locate and contact the other relatives and family members. Don't ask a grieving person what they want you to do for them or even how to get in touch with the other relatives. Try to obtain this information from other sources. Grieving people cannot think. They are fully involved in the grieving process and should be allowed all the space they need. Many times a hug can do more than anything else.

A surviving family member should not be left completely alone. Someone who is alone, with no relatives, friends or neighbors to stay with, should be with a compassionate caregiver. During acute states of anguish people can become temporarily suicidal.

Try to provide grieving family members with sufficient privacy to feel free to express their emotions.

Don't shield grieving persons from the body of the dead person. Many people need this last contact with the body to complete the grieving process and to resolve the loss. Denying this last contact opportunity can create long-term, unresolved psychological problems.

Supporting Children in the Event of a Death

The impact of death on a child can last a lifetime, so helping a child through this trauma should be a high priority. When adults become overwhelmed by a death in the family, sometimes children's emotional needs are not dealt with.

This problem is compounded by the fact that many adults find it difficult to talk to children about death. Children cannot be protected from the knowledge of death. Children are no different than adults in that they are not immune to the effects of death, and they also suffer from the loss. Thus children need to be included in the family's grieving so that they can heal their emotional wounds. They should be a part of all closure ceremonies.

A grieving child needs to receive undivided attention when his feelings come out. The adult with the child should stop his activity, look directly at the child and listen. When adults are able to openly express their grief, it can help free children to publicly express their own sadness.

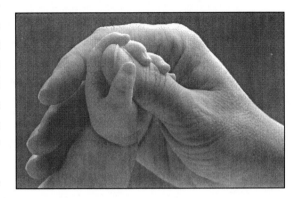

A child's response to grief may be different from that of an adult. Often, children's expression may be misinterpreted as behavioral problems. Unresolved grief in children can manifest as regressive behavior that can continue into adulthood.

A child's age and previous experience affect his understanding and perception of death. A child younger than two does not have much understanding of death. Between two and six, children display magical thinking. They may think that death is reversible and ask when the deceased is coming home again. From ages six to nine, a child will begin to comprehend the finality of death but may regress to magical thinking. They need to be guided compassionately during this transitional time. Children over the age of nine start to acquire a more mature understanding and do realize that death is irreversible.

The grief of children is often colored by fear of abandonment and fear that they too will die. Children need assurance of the continuing love and protection from other family members. Their major concern is that some person will still be there to take care of them and give them the unconditional love and security they need.

It is a mistake to tell a young child that a loved one is sleeping or has gone on a trip. This may make the child afraid of going to sleep, and in relation to going on a trip, the child might interpret this as being abandoned. The child can deal with the truth, simply stated by a family member, such as the loved one was so sick or so badly hurt that the doctors couldn't save them and so they died.

As with adults, children's guilt feelings always accompany grief. In a past fit of anger, a child may have once wished ill upon the deceased family member and blame himself. Even if the child does not verbalize this concern, he should be reassured that such a thing could never happen.

Should children be allowed to see the body? School-age children should certainly be allowed, but should never be forced. The decision should rest with the adults responsible for the child who best know his maturity and emotional status. If the death resulted in head or facial trauma or dismemberment, it may not be advisable.

Giving Support to a Dying Person

All of the advice about supporting those in grief due to the death of a loved one also applies to the dying individual who is going through his own personal grieving process. Dying individuals can become overwhelmed with anxiety. You can help these people come to grips with this situation by assisting them in the process of separating out and dealing with some of the individual strands that make up the overwhelming ball of anxiety. Try to determine if their major concern is for their own welfare or for that of another family member. Help this person sort out smaller worries. If some of these can be alleviated, the situation may not be so overwhelming.

In the first stage of dying, the individual mourns the impending loss of self. Shock and denial constitute the first phase, followed by an anger stage. The anger arises from feelings of frustration, injustice and resentment over one's situation. The third stage is bargaining with God or with some person who is perceived as being able to grant a temporary reprieve. This is an emotional respite, an attempt to postpone the inevitable. The fourth stage, depression, is a time of mourning past losses or failures, a time to grieve and cry. The last step is the stage of acceptance: a time of peace and contentment, but also of sadness. These stages are not clear-cut. One stage merges into the other and a regression into an earlier phase may occur at any time.

It is a mistake to assume anything from the facade that the dying person presents. The person who appears to be calm and in control may be just as frightened and unable to cope with his anxieties as the person who openly expresses his feelings. Communication is the key to dealing with grief. Good communication involves conveying a warm, receptive attitude; meeting the person's eyes with concern; or offering a touch. Supportive measures in themselves are not necessarily helpful or comforting —it is the way in which they are administered that makes a difference. Be compassionate, honest and sincere. Listening is one of the most effective things you can do.

If a dying person is alert and oriented, they need realistic support. Encourage the dying individual to express his concerns. Answer questions honestly and maintain as much hope as is reasonable. Dying individuals usually fear for the worst and honest answers may alleviate their worst fears.

The individual who is not able to talk but who is conscious or semiconscious should be assured that those taking care of him are aware of his concerns, and he should be given a realistic assessment.

Communication

Unconscious or semiconscious person may know what is going on around them. People should avoid making any negative comments based on the assumption that they can't be heard.

If the person is conscious but seems confused, calmly explain what is going on. Avoid using any phrases like "You will be okay" or "Don't worry." The person knows they are not okay and they do have good reason to worry.

One of a dying person's greatest fears is of dying alone. Have someone stay with them. When you are with the dying person, share yourself, let your eyes meet theirs, smile, and hold their hand. Make them feel that you care. Human contact means so much to the dying person.

Preparing Yourself for Death

When you are on the threshold of death your values seem to instantly change. Much of what was very important during life fades away and becomes very unimportant. A more profound set of values takes over.

To a certain extent, all of us relate to ourselves as our body. Most of the fear related to dying is due to this close identification with the physical body. In reality, the body is a vehicle that the real person, their spirit, inhabits or wears. The body is what is discarded at death.

There is not much instruction available on the subject of going through the process of death because very few people come back to tell about it. Some people view death as a veil that separates physical existence from spiritual existence. Passing through this veil is usually a one-way trip. Most how-to books are based on someone's personal experience. If everyone who tried to climb a particular mountain never came back, then that mountain would develop a particularly ominous and mysterious reputation.

However, recently there have been a number of books that contain testimonies of individuals who survived near-death experiences. Typically, these were people who were revived after drowning, cardiac arrest or death during surgery. Most of these recorded experiences contain common similarities that lend credence to their validity.

Some of the near-death survivors recalled a detachment from the body and a release from pain and confinement. This was described by one person to be "the most beautiful instant in the whole world." Many people recalled floating above their body with a conscious awareness of their own death. Some recalled viewing the body from a distance or even seeing it from many different directions at once. Most all experienced tranquility and delight, a timelessness, a limitless sense of freedom and the feeling of being an unencumbered spirit. There seemed to be a strong sense of having reached reality. There was a general experience of detachment from earthly concerns and a release from the burdens of mortal existence. Many people also relate experiences of being met by beings of light that conveyed to them, without words, great comfort and love. There are also references to traveling down a dark tunnel or a tunnel of light to a spiritual realm. In the final analysis, it appears that the moment of death is more distressing for family, friends and relatives than for the dying person.

A study reported that Near Death Experiences (NDE) were common in cardiac arrest survivors. Eighteen percent of 344 patients who were successfully resuscitated reported NDEs, according to the article "Near-death Experience in Survivors of Cardiac Arrest: A Prospective Study in the Netherlands" in *The Lancet Medical Journal* by Dr. Pim van Lommel with the Division of Cardiology at the Hospital Rijnstate in Arnhem. Some of them reported experiencing a "deep" NDE, which involved panoramic reviews of their life. They reported feeling what happened during life incidents, including experiencing the emotions of the other people involved. Some of these "deep" NDEs involved conversing with beings of light, meeting deceased relatives and viewing celestial landscapes.

Follow-up studies of these patients two and eight years after their NDEs indicated that the NDE caused significant changes in their lives. "People with NDE had a much more complex coping process: they had become more emotionally vulnerable and empathic, and often there was evidence of increased intuitive feelings. . . . Most of this group did not show any fear of death and strongly believed in an afterlife." The report also found that "most patients who did not have a NDE did not believe in a life after death."

Inner Peace in the Face of Death

In recent years a number of people have brought forth some unique insights regarding the topic of death in a way that is new to our Western culture. Eckhart Tolle, author of *The Power of Now* and *A New Earth*, is one of these people. In a radio interview on the show, New Dimensions, he was asked to comment on the grief people were feeling after the September 11 disaster. According to Tolle, the first step in dealing with grief is to acknowledge what you feel in the presence of death, perhaps deep sadness, perhaps loss. Something inside you dies with the death of another person. Do not deny this feeling but rather accept whatever arises. When you completely accept the feeling, allowing it and not denying it, the feeling remains but there is also a depth around this feeling. Don't run away from it internally. Accept that this is how it is. Surrender to death's reality and the acceptance of the fragile and impermanent nature of all forms.

In the face of death, when it is not resisted, the mind comes to a stop. The mind cannot make sense out of an event such as September 11, and for the most part, it cannot make sense out of any instance of death. In the presence of death, life doesn't make sense anymore. When the mind eventually gives up and the feelings are accepted, a place of deep inner peace can be felt beneath the sadness. This is the enormous deepening in oneself that happens in the presence of death, either your own approaching death or death very close to you. Once you have given up trying to interpret or judge, inner peace follows. Eckhart Tolle said, "People have reported in New York that many people seem to have changed. They suddenly talk to strangers. There is a greater softness that has come in, a greater humility that has come in, even love between strangers."

In regard to people who had near-death experiences he said, "There was an enormous sense of peace and serenity. And many have said that they wanted to tell those people who were in the room weeping, believing that this person was dying... 'There is no reason to weep because it is beautiful.' Something collapsed inside them, the whole structure of this mind-made self died. It can temporarily dissolve in the face of imminent death, and this is where this deep peace and serenity suddenly comes from because that is part of the essence of who you are, your innermost nature. In India it is sometimes called 'your natural state.'"

By understanding death, we are better equipped to face and conquer fear. Another benefit to contemplating the death process is that it helps people reevaluate their present-day priorities. What would you do differently today if you knew you were going to die tomorrow? On the threshold of death, many of the things that once were so important become trite and people lament things that they neglected during life.

CHAPTER 16

Terrorism

It seems inevitable that terrorist organizations will get, or now already have nuclear, chemical, and biological weapons and the means to deliver them. The good news is that many of the preparations you need for natural disaster will protect you in the event of terrorist threats. Water, food, shelter, and the ability to stand on your own are basic aids to combating terrorist attacks. Your knowledge of potential dangers, and a safe room for biological and nuclear threats, will be the primary additional needs to maintain your safety.

The main goals of terrorism seem to be to disrupt the public's sense of safety and to create feeling of vulnerability, fear and intimidation. By examining this subject and doing what we can to prepare ahead of time, we can successfully minimize the effectiveness of the terrorists' goals.

Biological Terrorism

Bioterrorism is the deliberate release of viruses, bacteria, or other germs with the intent to cause illness or death. The biological agents are usually found in nature, and are then changed to increase their ability to cause disease, make them resistant to current medicines, or to increase their ability to be spread throughout the environment. Biological agents can be disseminated through the air, the water, or in food. Terrorists might use biological agents because they can be extremely difficult to detect and do not cause illness for several hours to several days. Some bioterrorism agents, like the smallpox virus, can be spread from person to person and others, like anthrax, cannot.

History of Biological Warfare

The first recorded instance of biological warfare goes back several millennia when Scythian archers rubbed arrowheads in manure and rotting corpses to increase the deadliness of their arrows. The Tartars back around A.D. 1348 and 1349 used catapults to hurl the bodies of Black Plague victims (yersenia pestis) over the walls of the city of Caffa in the Ukraine. The Black Plague eventually spread from this city to Europe where it killed one-third to one-half of Europe's population. Bubonic plague has killed hundreds of millions of people during the span of recorded history.

It was the white man's diseases more than his technological edge that caused the decimation of the indigenous populations on the North and South American continents.

In 1754 American colonists intentionally distributed blankets from people infected with smallpox to the local Indian tribes. Due to their lack of immunity, the resulting smallpox epidemic killed 90 percent of the Indians exposed. Over the next 100 years the epidemic continued to move westward and facilitated the expansion of European populations on the North American continent. The Spaniards likewise brought smallpox and measles to Mexico and South America. The total death toll to Native Americans by white man's diseases is estimated to have been about 75 million.

The Japanese had an extensive biological warfare research program during World War II. Evidence indicates that the Japanese used biological warfare in China against the nationalist forces there. There is some evidence that the U.S. may have used bio-warfare in Korea.

The Current Threat of Biological Terrorism

"Biological terrorism is now considered by the U.S. Government to be a credible threat," says Dr. Christopher F. Richards of the Brigham and Woman's Hospital in Boston, Massachusetts. Early in the 1990s CIA Director John Deutch said that the threat of chemical and/or biological attack in the U.S. was "the most pressing intelligence challenge we face." According to John Gannon, a senior intelligence officer, chemical and biological weapons are a clear and present danger for the United States since "America's prestige and high profile as a global power make us the world's biggest and most dispersed target." According to former Defense Secretary William S. Cohen, "A lone madman or a nest of fanatics with a bottle of chemicals, [or] a batch of plague-inducing bacteria . . . can threaten to kill thousands." This threat has grown considerably since the 1990s.

In September of 1999 the Commission on National Security, sponsored by President Clinton and the U.S. Congress, released a report on the prospect of terrorism in the United States. This marked the beginning of an increased awareness and focus on the possibility of terrorist attacks on our nation. According to the report, "For many years to come, Americans will become increasingly less secure. America will become increasingly vulnerable to hostile attack on our homeland and our military superiority will not entirely protect us. Americans will likely die on American soil, possibly in large numbers. Threats to American security will be more diffuse, harder to anticipate and more difficult to neutralize than ever before." Unfortunately, this prophecy proved to be true in the tragedy of the attack on the World Trade Center in New York on September 11, 2001.

The greatest threat to the U.S. in the early part of the 21st century, "will not come from a military confrontation, rather it will come from an attack from within our borders from a single individual or group that has access to weapons of mass destruction," according to Colonel Dr. Edward Etizen Jr., with the U.S. Army Medical Corps at Fort Detrick, Maryland.

"A biological attack on a major city could approximate the lethality of a nuclear explosion," wrote Dr. Christopher F. Richards from the Brigham and Woman's Hospital in Boston, Massachusetts.

As we review these remarks made in the nineties with the fresh perspective of the 21st century, it is clear how accurate these comments were. The threat of biological terrorism is recognized throughout the world. "Weapons of mass destruction" is a phrase that even our school children know. Biological terrorism is now the theme of countless novels, movies and even TV shows.

In the aftermath of 9/11, a new arm of the government, the Office of Homeland Security was created. Information on biological terrorism is readily available on the Internet on the Red Cross site, the Center for Disease Control site and Ready.gov. There is no longer a debate over the possibility of biological terrorism. It has now become an acknowledged threat.

U.S. Government Bio-Warfare Response Plans

So what do we do about this seeming sword of Damocles that is hanging over the heads of humanity? The advice of Scott Lillibridge, director of the Bioterrorism Preparedness Program for the Center for Disease Control and Prevention is to "be prepared for the unexpected—whether it be a naturally occurring event such as a worldwide influenza pandemic or a deliberate release of anthrax by a terrorist." According to a taskforce of the American College of Emergency Physicians, "Without awareness and planning, a bioterrorism event may be unrecognized or dismissed as a natural epidemic until the scope of such a disaster becomes catastrophic." In July of 1999 Secretary of Defense William S. Cohen said, "The race is on between our preparations and those of our adversaries. We are preparing for the possibility of a chemical or biological attack on American soil because we must. There is not a moment to lose."

The U.S. Government has been doing more than just talking about the problem. According to Dr. Jeff Kopland, head of the U.S. Center for Disease Control and Prevention, the CDC has put together eight of what they call "Push Packages." Each Push Package includes 109 air cargo containers filled with antibiotics and related medical supplies that can be flown to any site of a bioterrorist incident in the U.S. within twelve hours. The CDC has also set up 81 labs around the U.S. that are equipped to test for six of the most likely biological agents that terrorists might use: plague, tularemia, botulin toxin, smallpox, ebola and anthrax. Hospitals and county emergency personnel are definitely becoming more aware of the potential of a biological terrorist attack. Individual counties in the U.S. are staging mock biological incidence training sessions for their emergency personnel.

This is encouraging. However, it will probably be too little, too late to be effective. It is easy to fall into the thinking that the "government has it all under control." If you go to the government-sponsored web sites it is clear that they are advising everyone to make their own individual plans for each potential disaster. They are not promising to do it all. As we saw in the aftermath of Hurricane Katrina, the government cannot protect you as well as you can protect yourself through prior planning and preparations.

Protecting Yourself from Biological Terrorism

If you live in a rural area, you are an unlikely target for a biological warfare attack. If you live in a heavily populated metropolitan area you need to seriously consider some sort of protective measure.

The big key to dealing with a contagious biological terror attack is isolation and the big key to being able to isolate oneself from the rest of the population is preparedness. If you have to go to the store or some government soup kitchen for food, you increase your risk of exposure. If you have to run all over town looking for asthma medications for one of your children, you increase your risk of exposure. Have a good food reserve, a dependable source of water, emergency medical supplies and a stockpile of any prescription medications you might require on a day-to-day basis.

Masks help prevent the spread of contagious disease.

A contagious biological outbreak could cause massive panic, quarantine and disruptions in the chain of supply. The terrorists may also try to target other infrastructures in the area of the attack in order to maximize disorder and impact. This could mean the possible sabotage of major power transmission lines and a resulting disruption of power. It could also mean the sabotage of municipal water systems and major water supply aqueducts. Power shortages and water shortages in a major city during a National Guard-enforced quarantine would only compound misery and chaos. In the event of a genetically altered biological attack when there is no effective vaccine, a good percentage of the police and health care workers may not show up for work. If you call 911 you might get a recorded message. Be prepared to take care of yourself.

Safe Rooms

One effective thing you can do for yourself and your family is to have some sort of certified, positive pressure nuclear, biological, and chemical air filtration system in your home with a HEPA quality filter. Most air filtration systems require electricity. In an all-out bio-warfare event the panic, hysteria and sabotage could potentially cause disruptions in the power supply. Any fool-proof air system should ideally have access to an independent back-up power system that won't be affected if the local utility fails. If you are dependent on that plug in the wall, your air filtration might not work. (See our chapter on Power Generation.) Residential, stand-alone in the room, air purifiers will not provide effective protection from a biological attack.

The Right Kind of Air Filter

An effective biological air filtration system draws air from the outside of the house via dedicated ducting, purifies the air and then pumps the purified air, under positive pressure, into the house or into some sort of relatively airtight isolation room. Positive pressure is a pressure greater than the normal air pressure outside of the house. A greater pressure inside the house causes the house, safe room or shelter to become very forgiving in terms of air leaks and infiltration from outside the house. The increased air pressure inside the house causes air to be continually forced out through any leaks in the exterior shell of the house, which includes windows, doors, vents and walls. Such a positive pressure air filtration system makes sure that only clean air gets into the house.

American Safe Room makes an ideal filter for use in creating a safe room for your home. The ASR-48-NBC Safe Cell is a portable positive pressure emergency air filtration system designed to offer protection in the event of a nuclear, biological or chemical attack when installed in a sealed room with a maximum volume of 48 cubic meters/1700 cubic feet (approximately a 14- by 15-foot sealed room with an 8-foot ceiling). This system is capable of giving adequate supply of filtered air for up to 8 persons. American Safe Room also makes an air filter that gives adequate supply of filtered air for up to 12 persons. Several families in one neighborhood could easily go in together on one safe room that would protect everyone in the group.

The system works by drawing in unfiltered air from outside your safe room through an intake vent that can be located in a wall, window, or door. The air passes through a bank of up to six filters certified for the entrapment of nuclear, biological and chemical (NBC) toxins, natural contaminants, and allergens. Then safe, breathable air is blown into your

protected space with just the right force to produce a slight overpressure in the room. This overpressure prevents toxins from migrating back into the shelter area through the cracks. This is the same technology used by the U.S. military to keep soldiers alive in their vehicles and command bunkers while in an NBC contaminated environment. The Safe Cell filtration unit meets the critical requirements of the Department of Army, U.S. Corps of Engineers.

The ASR filter is effective in the removal of the following war gasses: radioactive nuclear fallout, biological toxins, radioactive iodine, hydrogen cyanide, phosgene, mustard gas, sarin (GB), ricin, tabun (GA), VX, visicants/ blister agents.

A safe room with an ASR air filtration system is protected from avian influenza (bird flu),

An American Safe Room filter can be used to create a safe, toxin-free area in a room, vehicle, or portable shelter.

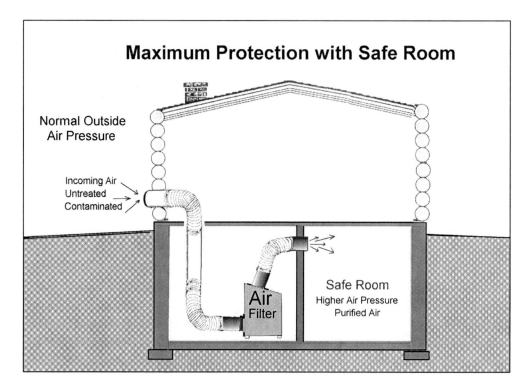

Maximum Protection with Safe Room

Normal Outside
Air Pressure

Incoming Air
Untreated
Contaminated

Air
Filter

Safe Room
Higher Air Pressure
Purified Air

SARS, or tuberculosis because the tested and certified HEPA will trap the droplet nuclei (bio-aerosol) produced by a contagious person. It would also be possible to turn this room into a negative pressure isolation room very quickly for a family member with the symptoms of these diseases. This would be done easily by moving one hose which attaches with a quick connection fitting.

The system operates from any standard 110–240 volt AC power source. In the event of a line power failure the ASR-48 Safe Cell has two emergency back up systems. The first back up is an automatic battery power system. In the event of a power outage, the power supply will revert to the user supplied 12-volt automotive battery, and when the power comes back on, it will automatically recharge the battery. The second back up is a hand-powered bellows that can be used to draw air through the filters if the battery is drained. This filter can be purchased through Yellowstone Trading.

In the event of an attack, close all windows and doors. Turn off the forced air central heating and air conditioning systems since these systems could draw contaminated air into the house. If you have a positive pressure air filtration system, don't completely seal up your safe room. The positive pressure will need somewhere to escape out of the room. The cracks under the door into your safe room will probably be adequate to accommodate air escape.

When Is It Safe to Leave Your Safe Room

A good battery-powered or hand-crank radio is an important item to have in your safe room. The reason again we emphasize battery-powered or hand-crank is because power failures due to either sabotage or the absence of service personnel could occur during an attack. Having a working radio makes it so that you do not have to go out of the house or safe room to find out if the coast is clear. Stay in your safe area until you hear a local report from the radio that indicates that it is safe to go outside. The telephone may continue to work, but 911 will be overwhelmed with calls and you will probably get a recording. A battery-operated radio scanner would be valuable. FRS or GMRS radios will allow you to communicate

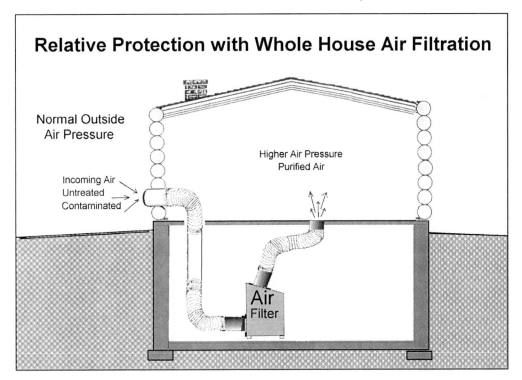

Relative Protection with Whole House Air Filtration

Normal Outside Air Pressure

Higher Air Pressure Purified Air

Incoming Air Untreated Contaminated

Air Filter

with neighbors. (See the Communication chapter in this book.)

If you do not have a positive pressure air filtration system then you must make every effort to seal up every possible leak into the house. Duct tape and caulk are your best resources in this area. In a normal house there is usually adequate air in the house to prevent the suffocation of its occupants, even when sealed up tightly. Suffocation in a confined area is not caused by an oxygen shortage, but by CO_2 build-up. Do not barricade yourself for an extended period of time in a confined absolutely airtight room that does not have an adequate source of purified fresh air. Suffocation could occur.

One alternative to an air filtration unit is to use a high-end vacuum cleaner with a HEPA collection filter to create positive air pressure in your safe room. Place your vacuum cleaner outside the safe room, but as far away from the room as the length of the hose will allow. You can buy extended lengths of plastic vacuum-type hose at home improvement centers and hardware stores. Connect the vacuum hose to the discharge side of the vacuum and run the other end of the hose through a hole in the wall into the designated safe room. Don't put the vacuum inside the safe room because the noise will drive you crazy. If you do put it in the safe room, you need to connect a hose to the intake side of the vacuum and run it through a hole in the wall out away from the safe room as long as it will reach. Either way, once you are done, plug in the vacuum, turn it on, go into your safe room and shut the door. This setup will work. It is not going to be as good as a real biological filter system, but it will be infinitely better than no filtration at all. Again, the electricity would have to be operating for the vacuums to work.

During the Gulf War when Saddam Hussein's army was firing Scud missiles at Israel, there was major concern that Iraq might be arming these scuds with chemical and biological weapons. What the Israeli population did, besides being issued a gas mask, was to construct safe rooms. These rooms were a designated room in a house that was lined and sealed off from the outside with 4–6 mil poly sheeting that comes in rolls. The sheeting was sealed at the edges with duct tape. The whole idea was to create a sort of makeshift clean room.

Other Considerations

In the event of a biological attack, essential services including law enforcement, emergency medical services, and water and food deliveries to local markets would probably be interrupted for a time. General preparedness is the key here. Have some sort of long-term food storage program, an alternative water source and an ability to purify it. Have a good first aid kit and some basic first aid training. And know how to protect your family and property if the police are too busy to help you.

Another consideration in preparing for biological terrorism is immune boosters. At this time the medical profession has little in its bag of tricks to deal with viral infections. Alternative medicine does have some anti-viral agents that show effectiveness under some conventional circumstances. It certainly wouldn't hurt to have these remedies on hand or use them routinely as a possible buffer. They may not cure a terminal case of smallpox, but in some cases they could make a significant difference in terms of who actually gets the virus and if they are in the percentages that live or the percentages that don't. The Medical chapter in this book discusses a number of the known natural anti-viral agents available.

What Is a Biological Weapon?

Biological agents are categorized into two basic groups: lethal agents and incapacitating agents. In other words, one category kills you and the other one makes you so sick you are unable to function or resist the enemy. Lethal and incapacitating agents are either bacterial, viral or toxins. Lethal agents include the following: Anthrax, Plague, Smallpox, Ebola, Ricin, and Cholera. Incapacitating agents include: Brucellosis, Q fever, mycoplasma, T-2 mycotoxins, Type B Enterotoxin and Equine encephalitis.

The characteristics of an effective bio-warfare agent are as follows. The agent must be infectious via aerosol deployment. The organism must be fairly stable in aerosol. Civilian populations must be susceptible to the infectious agent. The agent must have a high morbidity and mortality rate. The agent must transmit from person to person and must be difficult to diagnose and treat.

Bacterial Bio-Warfare Agents

Bacterial biological agents can be treated with antibiotics. Two important factors to successful treatment are early diagnosis and the availability of antibiotics.

Warning: The information that follows is not intended for individuals to use for any form of self-diagnosis or self-medication. The author, publisher, and distributors of this book accept no responsibility for people using or misusing the information in this chapter. The unsupervised use of antibiotics is dangerous. Antibiotics may cause fatal reactions due to allergy. This information should be used only in conjunction with the supervision of a medical doctor or other qualified medical health care personnel. Any independent use is at the risk of the user and should only occur as a last resort in a life or death situation where qualified/licensed medical help is not obtainable.

Typically, bacterial agents are classified either "gram-positive" or "gram-negative" due to their structure. Antibiotics are categorized based on their effectiveness against "gram-positive" or "gram-negative" bacteria or they are broad-spectrum antibiotics that are effective against both "gram-positive" and "gram-negative" bacteria. At the onset of a biological attack, it may be difficult to define the exact biological agent being used by the enemy and thus it may be hard to select the right antibiotic for treatment. The Soviet Union has been known to mix biological microbes into a "cocktail" weapon. Such a "cocktail" weapon would further confuse any clear diagnosis and accurate antibiotic treatment. For this reason the use of broad-spectrum antibiotics may be advised. Broad-spectrum antibiotics that deal with a wide range of both gram-positive and gram-negative biological agents may be the most effective option for treating people exposed to a biological attack with a bacterial weapon.

Allergic Reactions to Antibiotics

Antibiotics can save lives, but be aware that all antibiotics have dangers in their use. Some individuals are allergic to specific antibiotics. The initial symptoms of allergic reaction to an antibiotic can include skin rashes, itching, and breathing difficulties. Some reactions can become life threatening.

For more detailed information on specific antibiotics, dosages and their use, get a copy of the book, *Where There Is No Doctor.*

Viral Bio-Warfare Agents

There are a number of potential viral bio-warfare agents. These include Smallpox, Venez Equine Encephalitis, Viral Encephalitis and Viral Hemorrhagic Fevers. The really big bio-warfare concern is viral agents. Viral agents are contagious and presently there is no conventional cure for viral infection. If the viral agent you have been exposed to happens to be deadly, like smallpox, then all anyone can do for you is keep you hydrated and give you something for the pain. About 66 percent of the people who contract conventional smallpox will survive, with proper care. Smallpox immunization may provide some protection from conventional smallpox. It is likely that, to maximize effectiveness, terrorists would use a genetically altered strain of smallpox which the conventional smallpox vaccine will not protect against. It is equally likely that any viral agent used would be genetically altered or even possibly a genetically spliced virus such as Ebola-pox which has been developed in Russian bio-warfare weapons labs.

The book, *No Such Thing as Doomsday,* goes into greater detail on this subject of specific bacterial and viral agents and the potential treatment for each.

Nuclear Terrorism

In many areas, nuclear terrorism is enough of a real threat today to justify building a shelter. The possibility that a nuclear weapon will be used by terrorists increases annually. There are tens of thousands of nuclear weapons in national inventories, large amounts of weapons-grade uranium and plutonium potentially available to the black market, increasing dissemination of technical knowledge, and the existence of many countries that sponsor terrorism. The probability that terrorists will obtain

"Somewhere, sometime—but in this decade—somebody... is going to set off a nuclear weapon in deadly earnest."

—Rear Admiral Edward D. Shaefer Jr.,
Director of U.S. Naval Intelligence

possession of a functional nuclear weapon is increasing.

It is not within the scope of this book to cover the solutions to nuclear terrorism. If you are interested in this topic, get a copy of the book, *No Such Thing as Doomsday,* available from Yellowstone Trading.

Chemical Warfare

The use of chemical warfare is limited by the excessive bulk of the chemical agents. This restricts the size of the area which chemical agents can be applied to. Weather, wind and the practical limitations of dispersal would generally limit chemical weapons to use against concentrated targets as opposed to large geographical areas. Chemical weapons can be very effective against troop concentrations, military facilities, fortifications and highly populated areas. Chemical agents do not pose much of a threat to a civilian population except in very highly populated areas or near military facilities.

Protecting Yourself from Chemical Warfare Agents

The only way to protect yourself from chemical agents such as nerve gases, CN, mustard gas and others when you are outside in the open is the use of a protective suit and a military grade activated carbon gas mask. The suit has to be airtight, and the mask must fit snugly and filter all your air through canisters of chemicals that deactivate the chemical agent being used.

You can achieve a significant degree of protection from chemical agents by having a safe room in your house or other accessible location. See the section in this chapter where we discuss biological terrorism. For a more complete coverage of the topic of chemical warfare, get the book, *No Such Thing as Doomsday.*

CHAPTER 17
Biological Terrorism Scenario

Outskirts of Cheyenne, Wyoming

The day dawned bright and sunny like every other morning this fall but for some reason Dan Miller had an uneasy feeling in his stomach. Ever since September 11, 2001, his family's tranquility and security had disappeared.

His sister, an accountant working in Tower I of the World Trade Center, had been severely burned that day. Her agonized-though-determined recovery had a major impact on Dan and his family. Feelings of anger, frustration and helplessness alternated with awe, relief and gratitude that she was even alive.

The news was still peppered with stories of anthrax scares and attempted shoe bombings in this country as well as the usual suicide terrorist acts and continual warring in the Third World countries. The threat of World War III hung over everyone's head.

Dan flipped on the news as he brewed coffee. "There are three more potential smallpox cases reported today at the Cheyenne Memorial Hospital," said the local news reporter. "Spokesmen from the Center for Disease Control have issued an official statement saying that there is no need to panic yet, even though the figure for suspected cases nationwide has risen to 127. Everyone is advised to monitor their own health closely and report to their local hospital if they experience the following symptoms: fever with a chicken pox-like rash."

Suddenly Dan is very clear-headed. Adrenaline pumps through his system. "O my God! It's happened," he thought. "Okay. Keep calm. Let's think this through," Dan told himself as he went upstairs to get dressed and wake up the family. They had spent the past year preparing for just this sort of event. How well their plan would work remained to be seen.

Anaheim, California

Richard Hartman rolled over and punched the snooze alarm on the clock. 6:35 a.m. Thank God it's almost Friday. In thirty minutes he would be in the middle of rush hour traffic heading toward Costa Mesa to his financial advisor job. Richard went through his usual morning rituals: coffee and donuts, quick shower, dress and wake up the rest of the family. His teenage son and daughter and his wife started stirring around 7:00, just as he was leaving for work. He recognized the sound of his daughter's favorite CD playing as he closed the door behind him and headed to his car.

Easing into the flow of traffic on the crowded freeway, Richard settled into his seat and turned on a CD. The drive took over half an hour. At 7:30 Richard switched to the local news station, KNX 1070, to catch any important world events but mainly to hear the sports news about his favorite team. Nothing too exciting. A couple of suspected cases of smallpox reported locally (yeah, right) and the usual Israeli/Palestinian conflicts (when will these guys ever grow up). Impatiently he waited for the sports news.

At the office Richard quickly realized that something was up. Everyone else seemed to be taking this smallpox thing very seriously. It turned out to be happening across the entire country—35 out of the 50 states had one or more reported cases of suspected smallpox. Every single one of the 127 cases nationwide had been to Labor Day conventions, almost two weeks earlier. It was not just one convention but three different conventions at three different locations: Anaheim, Denver and Chicago. The Center for Disease Control seemed to be playing the whole thing down. Nothing to be alarmed over but anyone experiencing the symptoms must report immediately to the nearest hospital.

Day 1 – Wyoming

Dan, Beth and their four children lived on an acre of land just outside of Cheyenne. They had always been into gardening, chickens and milking goats. Then, ever since September 11 touched their lives so dramatically, they took the self-sufficiency idea a step further. It had seemed the best way to turn their concerns about the uncertain future into positive action, thus gaining a certain peace of mind.

They started out by ensuring that they would always have the essentials—water, food, heat, light, necessary medicines—in case anything happened to disrupt the flow of these necessities in the society at large. At first the task seemed overwhelming, but when they broke it down into manageable units, it was evident that this was truly something they could accomplish.

Water was not too difficult. They started out by storing two weeks of drinking water in their basement. One-half gallon per day per person. They had made the decision to replenish this water every month to keep it fresh. The date was marked on the calendar and they did this together as a family, each person pouring out their seven gallons of water and refilling them. This took less than ten minutes per person. Next they secured a small portable camping-type water filter and a stand-alone gravity feed water filter. Since they lived within walking distance of a year-round creek, they felt secure knowing they could always get good water to drink.

Food self-sufficiency hadn't been too hard to achieve either. Beth had always tried to buy in bulk, ordering monthly from a wholesale catalog many of the items the family ate regularly (grains, breakfast cereal, cheese, condiments, frozen hotdogs). Costco was a good place to buy applesauce, olives, nuts, spaghetti sauce, noodles and other things in large quantities. Having eggs and milk from their own animals helped a lot. With a deer in the freezer from hunting season last year and produce from their large garden, the family felt they could probably go at least a month without outside food if they really needed to. Right now they were in the process of putting up the early Fall harvest, freezing peas, spinach and green beans, storing potatoes, onions and various kinds of squash.

Over breakfast Dan, Beth and their kids discussed their plans. They agreed that it looked like an act of biological terrorism had occurred. The time to implement their plan had arrived. The plan was simple—isolation. Isolate themselves from all human contact until the threat of exposure to smallpox had disappeared.

The Millers home-schooled their children so this made things easy. Food and water were covered. They cooked with propane and heated with wood. If the epidemic caused enough of a disturbance in the local infrastructure to disrupt power, they had a small back-up generator and a bank of batteries that would cover their minimal electrical needs.

Both Dan and Beth worked out of their house on their small publishing business. No one had gone out at all yesterday. This was quite unusual for their active, large family and really quite a miracle. Everyone felt pretty sure they had not been exposed to the disease. They settled in for the long haul with considerable trepidation but also considerable hope.

Day 1 – California

As the day progressed, Richard wondered vaguely whether he should call his wife at work. She taught English at the local high school and Richard didn't want to pull her out of class. Conversation around the office about the smallpox cases died down as everyone was kept busy with work. Finally at 4:30, Ken, a rather conservative, politically aware co-worker moved around the office passing out xerox copies of an article he had just downloaded off the WorldNetDaily site. The number of cases had just skyrocketed to over 3,000 nationwide. It said the disease incubation period was just under two weeks with the contagious period peaking approximately two to three days after the fever begins, when the rash forms. Fortunately, by this time the person is usually too sick to be out in public, infecting others. Sneezing and coughing into the air is the way the disease is spread.

As Richard read the article he was quite amazed at the real facts about smallpox. There was actually no known cure. Whoa! He had thought modern medicine could cure just about anything. Of the total cases, one-third of the people would die. The two-thirds remaining would probably be disfigured and possibly blind for the rest of their lives. There was one potential reason for hope, he thought—vaccination.

On the way home Richard turned on his radio right away. He was amazed to find some stations still playing music. When he did locate some news, the whole smallpox epidemic didn't even sound like an epidemic. The news station reported the total number of cases at 392 and continued to put out reassurance that there was little to worry about. H-m-m-m. Two really different stories. Who should he believe?

Day 2 – Wyoming

Even though the Miller's isolation plan was simple, that didn't make it easy to implement, especially at the beginning. The children had liked the idea at first but by the second day they began to register what isolation really meant.

The rest of Cheyenne was just a little slower waking up to the reality of what had happened and so it was business as usual. "Why aren't you going to soccer practice today?" "What smallpox threat?" their friends asked. Ballet was still going on. The phones and electricity worked just fine.

It seemed a bit foolish to go to this extreme and the children put considerable pressure on their parents to modify the isolation plan so they could still do their favorite activities.

The second day was filled with arguments and indecision but in the end, Dan and Beth stuck to their plan, and by the evening news, they were glad they did. The real picture had finally begun to emerge.

Terrorists had simultaneously hit three of the largest convention centers in the country. Each convention was attended by nearly 5,000 people from all over the United States. The terrorists had put specially modified aerosol cans inside large soft drink cups for camouflage, and placed them in open trash cans around the convention center. Twisting the top of the can had started a time-delayed activation of the dispensing aerosol that contained the deadly smallpox virus. Supposedly, two individuals at each convention center could easily complete the setup and be out of the center before the cans began dispensing. Unbeknownst to anyone, the cans sprayed out an invisible mist of the deadly airborne virus.

The authorities were finally admitting to the public the seriousness of the situation as the 3,000 cases turned into 5,000 cases, about one-third of the total attendees at the three conventions. The known victims were in isolation wards in their local hospitals, but each one could have contaminated ten others, which in two weeks would bring the number of cases to 50,000. This, in turn, could mushroom into half a million cases in two more weeks.

The previous day's news reports had soothed people's fears with the reassurance that a mass inoculation and quarantine program was about to be started for anyone who had come within six feet of a smallpox victim.

However, after several fluid specimens taken from the victim's lesions had been tested at the Atlanta CDC lab, shocking news leaked out. This was a genetically altered form of the "India Strain," known to have been used in the Soviet Union's weapons program. The vaccine for standard smallpox would be completely ineffective.

It could take as long as two years to develop an immunization for this new strain.

As the Miller family sat around their TV following the news release, there was a stunned silence. The terrorist act was for real and their isolation plan was the only possible protection.

Day 2 – California

The day dawned hot and smoggy. Richard and his wife Carolyn had discussed the whole smallpox issue last night but they both relied on the major media networks for their information. And the media was saying there was nothing to worry about. "Everybody should carry on as usual. We have it all under control. Monitor your own health and report to the nearest hospital if you get a persistent fever."

So Richard went to work, Carolyn went to her teaching job, and their two teenagers went to school. Time stops for no one and "You gotta make a living."

In general, it appeared as if just about everyone else had the same idea; life seemed to be progressing as usual, both at work and at school. People were concerned and the whole smallpox thing was the exclusive topic of conversation but no one really knew what to do. Richard wished his friend Ken who had shown him the WorldNetDaily article yesterday was around to talk to. Ken hadn't come to work today.

Finally, the long, dragging day was coming to a finish and the Hartman family gathered around the TV to hear an update on the smallpox cases. They sat in stunned silence, unable to believe their ears. The number of smallpox cases nationwide had risen to 5,000. It was a genetically altered strain so the vaccine wouldn't work. The Anaheim Convention Center had been the target of a biological terrorist attack, now nearly two weeks ago!

As knots started forming in everyone's abdomen the news program described how officials planned to deal with the situation. The governor of California declared a state of emergency and was putting into effect the Model State Emergency Health Powers Act. The smallpox cases in Anaheim were second only to Chicago, 583. There was no way the hospitals could handle this many so a special isolation area had been set up at the L.A. Coliseum. All smallpox victims were being transported there by a specially trained tactical unit that wore white suits with air filtration systems.

This appeared to be mainly an isolation area where victims were left to die. Since there was no protection against contracting the disease, nurses, doctors and other medical staff were not showing up to work.

The most startling fact was that the whole Los Angeles area had been quarantined. The circle of the quarantine area checkpoints included everything north of Camp Pendleton Marine Base and Indio, everything west of Indio and Barstow, and everything south of Santa Paula and Camarillo. All ports had been closed. Bus and train stations were closed and the only air traffic allowed was military cargo aircraft bringing supplies into the area. No one was allowed to leave. No one was allowed to enter. Everyone was advised to stay in their homes.

Day 3 – Wyoming

Dan woke to the sound of knocking at the front door. "Who could that be?" It was just the UPS man leaving a package at the front door. As he drove away in his truck, it occurred to the Millers that they needed to put a note on the door stating, "Do Not Enter. This family is in isolation." They marveled at the fact that the rest of Cheyenne was still business as usual.

There were only nine smallpox cases in the city. By this evening the officials would finally realize that these cases could have infected ten other people each who could in turn infect another ten each. Without proper management the nine cases could mushroom into 900 within 30 days.

That evening the Cheyenne local government implemented quarantine for all potentially infected people and advised everyone else to stay at home. Although this was basically "too little, too late," unlike many larger cities nationwide, smallpox would not multiply out of control.

For the Miller family this day passed by uneventfully. They were grateful for their level of preparedness and felt secure that no one in their family had been exposed. They talked about the safe room they had in their basement. It was a room with an air filtration system that created positive pressure. This positive pressure kept out contaminated air without the room having to be 100 percent airtight. They had purchased the air filtration system for $1700. It had been difficult at the time to budget the money for this, but today they all realized it had been a good idea, even if only for the peace of mind it afforded everyone. They certainly hoped they wouldn't need to use it.

Day 3 – California

Things were looking rather grim for the Hartman family in Anaheim. The electricity and telephones were still on, which was good, but panic was spreading uncontrollably over the phone lines. Carolyn, Richard's wife, had learned that one of her fellow teachers at the high school had been at the Anaheim Convention over Labor Day and was experiencing smallpox symptoms. No one knew if he had been contagious the last day he was at the school teaching. If so, a large number of high school students as well as the other teachers had all been exposed. Everyone hoped the teacher had not been contagious.

What the L.A. quarantine would mean in terms of food for all the inhabitants was still to be determined. However, it was very clear that the government meant business in the quarantine issue. The current rumor going around indicated that one couple trying to sneak out at night had actually been shot at. No one knew for sure if they were wounded, dead or had successfully left the city. In any case, this was sobering news. The rest of the rumor indicated that under the current Model State Emergency Health Powers Act, the governor was asking all citizens to turn over their guns.

People had been told to stay in their houses but the Hartmans had needed food from the store. What they found when they went out was shocking. They couldn't buy gas anywhere because all the stations were closed and locked up. The local grocery store was locked, too. However, scared and hungry people don't always respect other's property. The windows had been broken and virtually all edible or usable products had disappeared from the shelves.

Day 15 – Wyoming

The Miller family survived the first two weeks of isolation without too much difficulty. There were many things they had to do without but, in general, their life was really not that much different. Dan and Beth were able to catch up on a lot of projects around the house and yard as their business had slowed way down due to the epidemic.

Thank goodness the phones were still working. This made their isolation much more tolerable. They could keep in communication with all their friends. This was especially helpful for the children.

The one thing that everyone felt really good about was that not only had they been able to carry on pretty close to normal, they had also been able to help out a number of their closest friends and neighbors. The other families were experiencing drastic food shortages and the Millers had an abundance of milk, eggs and garden vegetables, including bumper crops of potatoes and green beans. They prepared care packages and left them for their friends at the end of their driveway, just inside the gate. They knew this food made all the difference in the world.

Day 15 – California

The family was hungry, depressed and scared. Food shipments had been sporadic.

Carolyn came down with smallpox symptoms and was taken by the National Guard to the medical quarantine area in the L.A. Coliseum. Richard had tried to go visit Carolyn to see how she was doing but was greeted by corsetina wire and armed National Guard soldiers with gas masks on. The guards were impatient, telling him to move on. They said there was no means for him to get in contact with his wife at this time.

Richard and his two children were really hungry, hungrier than they had ever been before. There wasn't any more food in the house and they couldn't leave since public health officials had just placed a quarantine on their residence and family. There was yellow plastic police barricade tape across the front walk and a DO NOT ENTER sign duct-taped to the front door.

Health workers were supposed to be delivering daily food packages for the family and checking in to see if anyone else had developed symptoms. The lady that answered the telephone at the L.A. County Health Crisis Center said to be patient. She said county health personnel were overwhelmed and that additional federal troops were being brought in to help correct this problem.

100 Days Later – Across America

There have been hundreds of thousands of fatalities nationwide. The epidemic had had a devastating effect on the economy. The president of the U.S. declared a national emergency and implemented the Emergency Powers Act. The nation had been run by executive rule for the past three months with no set date for returning to representative government. The military had consolidated control of the inner city areas where riots, looting and arson had been a problem. The military was also handling food distribution to the larger cities. The government had resorted to creating civilian work brigades to help with clean up, burial and cremation of the dead and other health services.

Meanwhile, back in Cheyenne, things were beginning to return to normal. The Cheyenne Health Department had been able to stop the spread of smallpox with strict isolation of the victims and their contacts. Their success stemmed largely from the smaller size of their city and the lower number of smallpox cases. The city was able to maintain a basic level of functioning and had not needed government intervention. Even though the last few months had been extremely difficult for people who had no preparation or any degree of self-sufficiency, it had not been catastrophic as it was for many in the nation. They had survived, and hopefully were quite a bit wiser for the experience.

Appendix

Electric Motor Loads

Motor Size	Running Watts	Watts Required to Start Motor		
		Repulsion Induction	Capacitor	Split Phase
1/8	275	600	850	1200
1/6	275	600	850	2050
1/4	400	850	1050	2400
1/3	450	975	1350	2700
1/2	600	1300	1800	3600
3/4	850	1900	2600	–
1	1100	2500	3300	–

Note: Electric motors starting up can draw up to six times their normal running current. The table above may be used to estimate the watts required to start "Code G" electric motors. If an electric motor fails to start or reach running speed, turn it off to avoid equipment damage. Before attempting to use generator power, always check the wattage requirements of the appliance against the continuous rating of the generator.

Load Calculations

Description	AC or DC	Running Watts	Additional Starting Watts
Freezer or Refrigerator	AC	700	2200
Microwave Oven (625 watt)	AC	625	800
Dish Washer (cool dry)	AC	700	1400
Dish Washer (hot dry)	AC	1450	1400
Toaster (2-slice)	AC	1050	0
Toaster (4-slice)	AC	1650	0
Coffee Maker	AC	1750	0
Electric Frying Pan	AC	1300	0
Electric Kitchen Range (6" element)	AC	1500	0
(multiply each element in use) (8" element)	AC	2100	0
Kitchen Fan	AC	300	200
Dehumidifier	AC	650	800
Electric Blanket	AC	400	0
Electric Hot Water Heater	AC	4500	0
Clothes Washing Machine	AC	1150	2300
Gas Clothes Dryer	AC	800	1300
Electric Clothes Dryer	AC	5750	1800
Clothes Iron	AC	1200	0
Hair Dryer	AC	300 to 1200	0
Bathroom Fan	AC	100	0
Fireplace / Wood Stove Blower	AC	300	200
VHF Transceiver	DC	25	0
Television (color)	AC	300	0
Television (black & white)	AC	100	0
Radio Receiver	AC	50 to 200	0
Furnace Fan (Gas or Fuel Oil) - 1/8 HP	AC	300	500
Furnace Fan - 1/6 HP	AC	500	750
Furnace Fan - 1/4 HP	AC	600	1000
Furnace Fan - 1/3 HP	AC	700	1400
Furnace Fan - 1/2 HP	AC	875	2350
Well Pump - 1/3 HP	AC	750	1400
Well Pump - 1/2 HP	AC	1000	2100
Sump Pump - 1/3 HP	AC	800	1300
Sump Pump - 1/2 HP	AC	1050	2150
Vacuum Cleaner	AC	800 to 1100	0
Air Conditioner - 10,000 Btu	AC	1500	2200
Air Conditioner - 20,000 Btu	AC	2500	3300
Air Conditioner - 24,000 Btu	AC	3800	4950
Air Conditioner - 32,000 Btu	AC	5000	6500
Air Conditioner - 40,000 Btu	AC	6000	7800
Battery Charger - 4 amp	AC	90	0
Battery Charger - 10 amp	AC	2200	0
Battery Charger - 15 amp	AC	380	0
Battery Charger - 30 amp with 200 amp boost	AC	650/3600	0
Battery Charger - 60 amp with 250 amp boost	AC	1500/5750	0
Battery Charger - 80 amp with 275 amp boost	AC	2000/6800	0
Battery Charger - 100 amp with 300 amp boost	AC	2400/7800	0

Electrical Demand Planning Worksheet

AC/DC	Appliance	Qty		Watts Per Hour (Volts x Amps) Multiply by 1.1 for AC		Hours in Use Per Day	Total Daily Wattage
			X		X		
			X		X		
			X		X		
			X		X		
			X		X		
			X		X		
			X		X		
			X		X		
			X		X		
			X		X		
			X		X		
			X		X		
			X		X		
			X		X		
			X		X		
			X		X		
			X		X		
			X		X		
			X		X		
			X		X		
			X		X		
			X		X		
			X		X		

Maximum AC Wattage at One Time				Total wattage (Watt Hours) Per Day	

Total Wattage Per Day		Battery Inefficiency Factor		Total Adjusted Daily Wattage
	X	1.25	=	

AC Loads Which Will Run Directly Off the Generator

Appliance	Qty	Wattage Per Hour	Hours Per Day	Watts Per Day

Battery Sizing Worksheet

Total Adjusted Daily Wattage (from Electrical Demand Worksheet)	
System Voltage ? (12 or 24)	÷
Total Amps Per Day	=
Desired Capacity of Battery Power in Days	X
Required Amp Capacity for Battery Bank	=
Depth of Battery Discharge – DOD	÷ %
Total Amp Hour Battery Capacity	=

Notes and Calculations:

_____

_____

_____

_____

_____

_____

AC Cable Sizing Chart

Current Amperes	Load in Watts		Maximum Allowable cable Length				
	120 Volts	240 Volts	#8 Wire	#10 Wire	#12 Wire	#14 Wire	#16
2.5	300	600	–	1000 ft.	600 ft.	375 ft.	250 ft.
5	600	1200	–	500	300	200	125
7.5	900	1800	–	350	200	125	100
10	1200	2400	–	250	150	100	50
15	1800	3600	–	150	100	65	–
20	2400	4800	175 ft.	125	75	50	–
25	3000	6000	150	100	60	–	–
30	3600	7200	125	65	–	–	–
40	4800	9600	90	–	–	–	–

DC Wire Loss Table - 24 Volts

Amps in Wire	Wattage at 24 Volts	Wire Size									
		#14	#12	#10	#8	#6	#4	#2	1/0	2/0	3/0
1	24	226	350	550	900	–	–	–	–	–	–
2	48	113	175	276	450	710	–	–	–	–	–
4	96	50	88	138	226	356	–	–	–	–	–
6	144	38	60	88	150	238	376	–	–	–	–
8	192	28	43	72	113	178	288	–	–	–	–
10	240	23	35	58	90	143	226	360	–	–	–
15	360	15	23	35	60	95	150	240	386	–	–
20	480	10	18	28	50	73	113	180	290	360	458
25	600	9	14	23	35	58	90	145	230	290	366
30	720	8	12	18	30	48	75	120	193	240	304
40	960	–	–	14	23	35	58	90	145	180	228
50	1,200	–	–	12	18	28	46	73	115	145	183

DC Wire Loss Table - 12 Volts

Amps in Wire	Wattage at 24 Volts	Wire Size									
		#14	#12	#10	#8	#6	#4	#2	1/0	2/0	3/0
1	12	113	175	275	450	710	–	–	–	–	–
2	24	56.3	87.5	138	225	335	576	900	–	–	–
4	48	25.0	43.8	68.8	113	178	288	450	725	900	–
6	72	18.8	30.0	43.8	75	119	188	300	481	600	760
8	96	13.8	21.3	36.3	56.3	88.8	144	225	363	450	570
10	120	11.3	17.5	28.8	45	71.3	113	180	290	360	457
15	180	7.7	11.3	17.5	30	47.5	75	120	193	240	304
20	240	05.0	08.8	13.8	22.5	36.3	56.3	90	145	180	229
25	300	04.5	07.0	11.3	17.5	28.8	45	72.5	115	145	183
30	360	03.8	06.0	08.8	15	23.8	37.5	60	96.3	120	152
40	480	–	–	07.0	11.3	17.5	28.8	45	72.5	90	114

Effects of Radiation on Water

A total of 18 inches of earth will filter all radioactive dust particles out of rain and surface water penetrating into the ground. Well water would be unaffected by radioactive fallout as long as the well casing was not open at the top. If stored water is enclosed in sealed containers, any fallout that has settled on the container can be cleaned off before opening. The water in any such container can be safely drunk.

If water is exposed to radioactive fallout, it does not necessarily make the water itself radioactive. The fallout does not contaminate the water chemically, but only through the presence of particulate material which can be removed by filtering. Even if the container is open and has been contaminated with radioactive fallout dust particles, the water can be filtered and safely used. Any material capable of filtering out dust particles may work, such as milk filters, multiple layers of paper towels or layers of cloth from a bed sheet. A conventional water filter or purification system is the best instrument to use.

Effects of Radiation on Food

If food is exposed to radioactive fallout, it does not necessarily make the food itself radioactive. If food is enclosed in sealed containers any fallout that has settled on it can be cleaned off before opening the container and contents can be safely consumed. Food can be safely grown in fallout-contaminated soil a month after the fallout occurred.

Foods such as clams, mussels, and organs of mammals should not be eaten during periods of radioactivity because they act as filters and concentrate contaminants. Livestock can be butchered and eaten if the meat is boned and the fat is discarded. Milk from dairy cattle grazing on contaminated ground will be unsafe to drink for 30 days after a nuclear event. After 30 days, the milk can be safely used. Root crops, seeds, fruit and berries grown in contaminated soil should not be eaten because of the water-borne contaminants they absorb through their roots which then become concentrated in the plant. A second crop would be safe to eat.

In case of impending radioactive fallout, it would be good, if material and time allow, to cover garden areas with plastic sheeting. This will catch and keep fallout particles from soaking into and contaminating the earth. The plastic can be removed once the fallout is over and radiation levels are low enough to be considered safe. This garden area can be immediately used for planting and any subsequent crops safely eaten.

Resources

Preparedness Supplies

Yellowstone Trading
    1716 S. Willson Ave.
    Bozeman, MT 59715
    (800) 585-5077
    email: orders1@yellowstonetrading.com
    www.yellowstonetrading.com

Major Surplus and Survival
    435 West Alondra Blvd
    Gardena, CA 90248
    (800) 441-8855
    www.MajorSurplus.com

The Survival Center
    PO Box 234
    McKenna, WA 98558
    (360) 458-6778
    www.survivalcenter.com

American Civil Defense
    11576 S. State St., Suite #502
    Draper, UT 84020
    (800) 425-5397
    www.tacda.org

Lehmans
>One Lehman Circle
>PO Box 41
>Kidron, OH 44636
>(877) 438-5346
>www.Lehmans.com

Medical and Health Supplies

Moore Medical Corp.
>(800) 234-1464
>www.mooremedical.com

Dixie USA
>(800) 233-3668
>www.dixieusa.com

First Responder Supplies
>(918) 427-3600
>www.firstrespondersupplies.com

Jeffers Vet Supply
>(800) 533-3377
>www.jefferspet.com

Dr. Richard Schultz
>(800) HERB-DOC
>www.herbdoc.com

Recommended Reading

Making the Best of Basics, James Stevens (food storage, menu planning, and food preparation)

Encyclopedia of Country Living, Carla Emery (available from Yellowstone Trading)

Where There Is No Doctor, David Werner (available from Yellowstone Trading)

Brady Emergency Care, Grant, Murray and Bergeron

Stay Prepared! Contact Us.

We want to hear your comments and questions. Please e-mail us at orders1@yellowstonetrading.com.

Yellowstone Trading, in partnership with Yellowstone Publishing, is a source for the products we recommend in this book. For more than a decade, we have searched the market for the best preparedness items and have tried out nearly all of them personally. We are confident that the time and effort we have put into this research will save you time and effort.

Find out more about the products recommended in this book by visiting our web site at www.yellowstonetrading.com, or call (800) 585-5077. Our company provides the latest emergency preparedness information, online resources, and superior products. We offer the highest level of customer service that only a small company can give. Your purchases support our family-run business and our preparedness advocacy efforts.

For the latest information and products, sign up for our free newsletter on our web site. It provides updated information, featured columns, and how to best prepare for threats as they develop around the world.

Reading this book is a great first step towards peace of mind. In these uncertain times, continue on this path of increased security by letting us help you prepare.

About the Author

Arlene Hoag has 20 years experience homesteading and raising a family at the edge of the Montana wilderness. She earned a BA in Psychology from the University of California at Santa Cruz and then went on to earn

Arlene Hoag

her teaching credential. In 1985 she moved to Montana and found it to be a great place to raise her family. This was the start along her path of self-sufficiency. She learned that this path didn't mean having to provide everything necessary to live on without going to the store, but it was all about learning how to take care of oneself and others for a while during an unforeseen emergency.

Twelve years ago she chose to get involved in the preparedness field because of her desire to help others acquire the peace of mind that comes from knowing you are ready for possible emergencies. She shares that knowledge with her customers as owner of Yellowstone Trading Company, which she manages with her grown daughter, Bethany. The company provides preparedness equipment and supplies, including a 72-hour survival kit and long-term food storage programs.

Arlene is the co-author, with Philip Hoag, of their first book, *No Such Thing as Doomsday*.

LaVergne, TN USA
19 February 2010

173649LV00002B/1/P